Michmash frowning in rocky strength

A Man of Valor

CHAPTER I

A Perilous Situation

MICHMASH, frowning in rocky strength, stood crowned with light by the morning sun. The broken line of her steep cliffs rounded in from the northwest, where they opened in the pass of Beth-Aven, and swept toward the east, to the Jordan valley. Facing these cliffs, a mile distant, rose the equally abrupt face of the heights of Gibeah, to the west and south of which rolled up the hills that held Ramah, and Gibeah, and Nob, and Jerusalem, the stronghold of the Jebusites.

Over against each other, like two opposing hosts waiting for the signal to combat, stood these rugged, rock-browed hills. Their somber limestone faces cast in deeper gloom the margins of the vale below, from which the springtime's rushing torrents had withdrawn, and left, in their stony channels, no barrier to the contending forces.

And, indeed, there was conflict impending,— if not between the forces of the hills, between the men that lay encamped upon their summits. On the one side lay Geba ("The Hill"), from which a garrison of the invading Philistines had recently been expelled. The smitten band had fled to the opposite heights of Michmash, and, there reënforced, now lay watching developments upon the other side.

Israel was in sore trouble. The little victory at Geba had but served to draw out their enemies in greater number, and with more destructive designs. Three companies of spoilers went out from the great camp of the Philistines. Toward the south, the west, and the north, their raids extended to Dan, to Judah, and even, perhaps, through Ephraim to Manasseh; but their hand was heaviest upon Benjamin.

A strong, warlike people, a nation selfish in spirit, determined in purpose, and aggressive in action, they were the dread of all surrounding kingdoms. Their confederacy of five principal cities had never been completely broken by any conquering power; and when the far-reaching hand of Egypt had been withdrawn, and their neighbors were weakened by division and petty strife, they assumed a leading part in the affairs of Canaan and Phenicia.

The invasion of the Israelites at the time of the Conquest, while in the main successful in all other quarters, was stopped in this southwestern corner of the land by the iron chariots and the spears of the giants that lived in Gaza and Ashdod and Ashkelon and Gath and Ekron.

The powerful Israelite tribe of Dan had been forced by them to divide its people and pass far to the north to find a new home; Shamgar had made headway against them for a time, and delivered Israel from their oppression; Samson had fought their men and been conquered by their women; and Samuel had smitten and awed them. But now the prophet was old, and his sons made judgment to miscarry, so that Israel, discouraged and apostatizing, had again invited an easy conquest.

The people, feeling, in their separation from God, the lack of power to make headway against their enemies, had demanded a king, that they might be like the nations about them; and, under solemn protest from their divine Ruler, whom they thus rejected, the king was given. Saul of Gibeah, notable among the men of Israel for his stature, beauty, and commanding presence, had won the hearts of the people by his masterly relief of Jabesh-Gilead, when it was besieged by the Ammonites, and his hewing to pieces the army of Nahash, their king. Yet not two years of his reign had passed before the Philistines were practically masters of all the south country. They exacted heavy tribute of the vine-dressers, the herdsmen, and the tillers of the soil. They took what pleased them, and smote those who would resist. And, lest the desperate people should rise in revolt, they took from them every weapon of war, and forbade any smith to ply his trade in Israel. A file to sharpen his plowshare, his ax, and his goad, was the only smith's implement the Hebrew might possess. Yet the people were not wholly unarmed. The sling with which the shepherd practised in his lonely hours on the hill, or with which he drove away the wild beasts that threatened his flock, could be pressed into service for more terrible work if occasion should require; and the bow, that universal weapon, was in the hands of every man. Childish hands bent the lithe willow for the reed shaft, while more practised fingers carved the cypress in leisure hours; so that, even if removed by the Philistine conquerors, the bow could quickly be replaced to every fighting-man. But none were there who could smite the sickle to a straighter edge, or forge the plowshare into sword. So it came to pass that only with Israel's king and his son was there found sword or spear in the day of battle.

A Man of Valor

And the Philistines were drawing their lines tighter about the new-made monarch. They held the West, and they had passed around to the north and seized the heights of Michmash, cutting the line of communication between Saul and the powerful tribesmen of the North. Behind him were the unconquered Jebusites in their mighty stronghold; and his only remaining line of retreat lay toward the wilderness, where prowled the vagrants of Amalek, and into which the forces of Moab and Ammon would quickly be thrown to smite him in his distress. Thus the Philistines reckoned that a short time would suffice to crush this upstart king, who threatened to wrest their slaves from their grasp.

Then came Geba. This, their most advanced post, was surprised and taken by a few Israelites under a mere stripling, Jonathan, eldest son of King Saul. The deed sounded the tocsin of deadly strife. All Israel heard that Saul had smitten the garrison of Geba, and that Israel was held in abomination by the Philistines. Saul called for the people to come out to his help; and from every possible point they gathered to his standard at Gilgal.

This was a sacred spot to every Israelite. It was the first camping-place of the people when they had passed over Jordan under Joshua; here stood the monument of twelve great stones, taken from the bed of the river as a memorial the day that the Lord piled up its waters to let Israel pass over dry-shod; it had been the headquarters and rallying-place in times of national danger for many generations; here Saul himself had been settled in the kingship by the voice of all the people, after the victory of Jabesh-Gilead. The memories of the place were such as to inspire patriotism and courage; and the call to arms was answered by many thousands from the surrounding country, and even from the over-river district of Gilead. But what a motley array they presented! The vine-dresser came with his pruning-knife, the reaper with his sickle and his fork, the herdsman with his sling, the plowman with his long spear-like ox-goad; and thus they formed themselves to meet a well-appointed enemy, countless in number as the sands of the seashore, with six thousand horsemen and thousands of chariots of iron.

It was a situation to appal the stoutest of heart; and these poorly prepared hillsmen of Judah and Benjamin, these herdsmen of Gad and Manasseh, were none too courageous. Besides, the place had no natural means of defense. It was close to the

A Man of Valor

point of greatest danger, where the Philistines could strike most easily. It was on the plain, where the cavalry of the enemy would have their greatest advantage against the footmen of Israel, and where the great war-chariots, with scythe-decked wheels, could mow death-strewn swaths through devoted ranks.

Saul's host the first days numbered thousands, but as the terror grew with succeeding hours, the army dwindled and shrank. As the situation forced its fears upon their minds, the people hastened to hide themselves in caves and pits, among the rocks of the hills, and in the thickets of the woods. Some, stricken with hopelessness, passed over the Jordan to the wilderness and the rock fortresses of Gilead, exiling themselves, in despair of any success that could come to the arms of Saul. Still others, baser of soul, purchased to themselves present safety by deserting to the camp of the Philistines, forsaking their country and their God for the miserable boon of a life lengthened out in abject servitude and fear.

In this dire strait, Saul called for Samuel the seer to help. The great crisis of his kingdom had come, and he remembered the words spoken by the prophet in the day when he anointed him king. Samuel, looking forward to the certain crisis that would come both in the experience of the nation and in the life of its king, saw the encroachments of their enemies upon the Hebrew people, and the siege that the great Enemy would lay to Saul's soul; saw the narrowing of the conflict as point after point was yielded by each; saw the concentration of both dangers at this decisive hour; and, looking upon the young man to whom he had just declared his selection as king, he pointed out the course in which lay salvation to people and prince. The saving of each should come by faith, not by personal action; by waiting in trust, not by striking in haste. "Thou shalt go down before me to Gilgal," he said; "and, behold, I will come down unto thee, to offer burnt-offerings, and to sacrifice sacrifices of peace-offerings; seven days shalt thou tarry, till I come to thee, and show thee what thou shalt do."

Saul had fulfilled the first part of these directions, and now he must endure, with his people, the second part of the test. After their gathering together at Gilgal, the army must wait a faith-testing week to hear the directions of God. The days dragged slowly to Saul and his fear-stricken men, momentarily expecting attack from their enemies; and the desertions increased.

Saul, as commander and king, might, in this

A Man of Valor

extremity, have proved himself as powerful in moral force as he was great in military tactics. He might have added to his repute as general a renown as statesman. He could have held the people to his standard and camp and swayed the thousands of troubled minds by the power of his faith. That would have been a greater and nobler deed than a brilliant victory on the battle-field. If his countenance had every morning shown a cheerful confidence in the outcome of the impending conflict; if he had spoken to the people words of hope and trust in the power and love of God; if he had inspired them by his every action to wait in confidence for the coming of God's spokesman, he would have proved himself indeed a king, and would have vindicated his selection by the people and by God. But while the existence of the kingdom of the nation was trembling in the balance, the kingdom of his soul was flinging out the white flag from its every stronghold. In the moral struggle that he had to wage he was losing, and through that loss he was endangering his visible dominion.

So seven suns set, and seven times the stars faded, while Saul watched his army melt away, and put forth no staying hand. Impatiently he waited for the promised coming of the prophet, and attributed all the gloom and desertion to Samuel's absence. But the appointed morning came; it wore on and passed; and yet Samuel had not arrived; for God's providence had detained him. Saul, whom the inactivity was torturing, could not wait a moment beyond the set time; but, rash and headstrong, and determined by any means to stop the thinning of his ranks, he called for an ephod, the distinctive badge of a priest, and himself, with unconsecrated and unholy hands, usurped the sacred office, and began to offer up the sin-offering and the peace-offering for his people,— a sin-offering that was itself a sin, and a peace-offering that banished peace.

The offering of sacrifices by fire was a solemn ervice, in which none might participate unprepared. Prayerful heart-searchings were to be made before the sinner came to confess and offer the sacrifice; for the lamb slain and burnt upon the altar typified the sacrifice of the coming Christ, whose death should avail for the pardon of the sinner. With reverent mind the worshiper must come to this service, by faith grasping the promise of a coming Saviour, if the ceremony was to be of value. While in the beginning God had provided that the head of each family should act as its priest to offer the sacrifices, in Israel

A Man of Valor

he had set apart as his ministers one tribe, the Levites, and of them the family of Aaron, to act as priests for the whole nation. To them alone belonged the sacred rites. Samuel was a Levite and a priest.

But Saul, not used to reverent thought, saw in the sacrifice little spiritual significance, and attributed to the ceremony itself the effect of securing the favor of God, as though the Lord's justice would be satisfied because of the value of the gift and the giver's act of homage. Seeing in the service only an act which in the present instance might insure courage and loyalty in the ranks, he determined, with his characteristic headiness, to take the responsibility upon himself, and did not scruple to stand in the armor of a man of war to officiate at the altar of the God of peace.

Scarcely had he finished offering the first sacrifice, when Samuel came. In response to the prophet's inquiry, " What hast thou done? " Saul presented the excuse of expediency and necessity for his transgression. " Because I saw that the people were scattered from me," he said, " and that thou camest not within the days appointed, and that the Philistines gathered themselves together at Michmash; therefore said I, The Philistines will come down now upon me to Gilgal, and

I have not made supplication unto the Lord; I forced myself therefore, and offered a burnt-offering." But the man of God sternly rebuked his presumption, and declared that by his wrong course he had proved himself unworthy of the trust God had reposed in him, and that his kingdom should not continue. The Lord had sought him a man after his own heart, a man of unwavering trust and of perfect obedience, and he had not found him in Saul. Samuel returned to his home in Ramah, and Saul turned to his army. They numbered six hundred!

Saul felt himself abused and wronged by this course of the prophet. In his own eyes he had done a necessary and a creditable thing, and he could see no reason for displeasure to rest upon himself. Resentful and rebellious, and bent upon justifying his course, he declared in his heart that if Samuel would thus desert him, he would become independent of Samuel. He would play the politician, and against the power of the prophet pit the venerable authority of the priests. The tabernacle of God was pitched at Nob, then the sacred city of the nation, and there the high priest, Ahimelech, with his family and others, was in attendance upon the holy service. To him, therefore, Saul sent, and desired him, as a patriot and the highest representative of the religion the existence of which was now threatened in the peril of the nation, to come to him with the sacred symbols, and by his presence inspire the hearts of the people.

Ahimelech came, clothed with the sacred vestments; and to the authority of the king was added the priest's example and such protection as his presence might be expected to bring. Yet it was a time of foreboding; for, despite the ready response of the priest, the people, knowing the king's irregular course in sacrificing, and his evident disfavor with the man of God, felt themselves under the shadow of impending evil; and Saul, not daring to remain longer in his exposed position, broke camp at Gilgal, and advanced to take a position in the hills. Though troubled in mind, and harassed by the dangers of the situation, he showed his dauntless spirit, as ever, by choosing a post of danger. Geba, once taken, must not be given up, and there, under a pomegranate tree upon the brow of the hill,— Migron, "a precipitous place,"— he pitched his bivouac.

But, brooding in disquietude and anger, he took no steps to hearten his men, or to move against the Philistines. Days still passed without result, while the land waited for the tide of the heathen invasion. Yet a conflict was coming, the inception of which no man could have foretold, and the result of which no man would then have dared to credit. The sun rose upon Michmash to see a wondrous day.

CHAPTER II

Not by Many, but by Few

LET us, before the gleams of the rising sun leap over upon the encampment around the pomegranate tree on Migron, and awaken to dull activity again the few followers of Saul, steal near to view the order of this little band, the forlorn hope of Israel. Upon the precipice opposite the heights of Michmash, where the Philistine army lies encamped, the king has struck his tent. The faint light of the dawning day reveals around his lone pavilion the sleeping forms of the few hundred who yet cling to the royal standard. A sentry in front, toward Michmash, and a second in the rear, looking toward the country of Philistia, stand, each leaning upon his spear, listless and with dejected countenance, yet, with the eagle eye of the Benjamite, still watchful for distant signs of danger.

The scanty dew of the warm night glistens, yet undried, upon the prostrate forms of the soldiers. No signs of life come from the tent where the haunted monarch sleeps alone. But now at the outer border of the encampment there is a slight stir, as one of the sleepers, doubtless aroused by uneasy thoughts, wakens and rises. Alert and self-possessed at the moment of wakening, he runs his eye over the sleeping throng, and then glances out over the swales of the valley below, and across to the hostile camp on the opposite side. For a few moments he stands lost in thought; then, stooping, he gently rouses a youth who has slept by his side, and beckons him to follow. Past the sentry they go, with a slight recognition from either, down the slope of the lesser hill, and pause in the wood at its base.

As they face each other, let us study more closely the person of the first. His dress, though the simple one of a soldier, betokens high rank. His armor is that of the time. A coat of mail, formed of small but heavy plates of brass linked together, covers his body from shoulders to thighs; below, a purple tunic of fine-twined linen escapes from under his mail. His legs are protected in front by lighter greaves of brass, while upon his feet are bound simple leathern shoes, or sandals, whose worn condition tells of a recent life of activity and adventure. His arms are bare, save for the short armlets of his brazen coat and the little longer sleeves of his tunic, which do not conceal the swelling of the muscles as he gestures. But upon his wrists, insignia of his rank, we see curi-

This is Jonathan, son of Saul

ously wrought bracelets of gold; and the lacings of his sandals, though soiled and frayed, show still the loving workmanship of a cultured daughter of Israel.

Not long, however, in sight of the frank and manly face, can notice be given to his dress. The glances of his bold yet modest eye draw the attention like a magnet. The oval of the Israelitish face is modified somewhat in his profile by the firmer setting forward of the chin, a feature that speaks determination and quiet will. Above straight brows, his forehead rises evenly, a forehead tanned by exposure up to the rim of his silver helmet-cap, from beneath which escape the black, wavy locks whose beauty has even been sung in Holy Writ.

This is Jonathan, son of Saul, heir to the kingdom, and the glory even now of Benjamin and almost all Israel. He it is that smote the garrison of the Philistines at Geba; under his hand has been placed by the king a third of all the nation's little army; and his ardor and enterprise are answered in the devotion of his men. Yet he is but a youth. The Oriental matures early, and becomes while yet in his teens an adult in appearance. In Israel the youth who at sixteen or eighteen was almost a boy, in a year or two would appear a bearded man; for the razor was seldom used, and the beard was held almost sacred in the eyes of the people. Yet scarcely has the down of earliest manhood appeared upon the lips of this young man. Tall and well formed, like his father, he is yet of slighter build, and his lithe form contrasts well when set beside the heavier though yet energetic person of the king. Now, as he talks, the animation of his countenance and his whole form set off to advantage the grace of his person, and draw the eye in admiration.

His companion is his armor-bearer. Somewhat more slightly protected himself by armor, usually he carries upon his left arm, or sometimes slung upon his back, the heavy shield of his master; the bow and the quivers, the heavy spear and the javelin, are also borne by him when not in use. He has no sword; for such is the present poverty of Saul's little army; and now he carries none of the heavy armor or weapons of his master; for they are embarking on an enterprise of hazard that will require the lightest burdening possible.

What has called them forth at this early hour, before their companions can mark their departure? Listen, and we shall hear. Up yonder lies the little camp of the forsaken king, a few faith-

A Man of Valor

ful followers alone clinging to his fortunes, his mind a prey to the lashings of injured pride and stinging conscience. The hordes of the heathen are beginning to stir in the distant camp at Michmash. Will to-day see the onsweep of their resistless march, and Israel's hope as a nation finally blotted out? Where are these two bound? and upon what errand?

We catch the words of the young prince as he answers the question that speaks from the eyes of his companion: "Come, and let us go over to the Philistines' garrison, that is on the other side." What! Does the prince of Israel seek to desert in this hour of evil and distress? And does he think that enemy whom he slew at Geba will welcome him into their camp? They might, for even yet there is hazard to them when they meet the lion-king at bay. But listen as he speaks again: "Let us go over unto the garrison of these uncircumcised: it may be that the Lord will work for us." The eyes of the armor-bearer kindle as they catch the shining of his master's. But what shall two do? And the answer, ringing with sublime faith, comes in the closing words: "For there is no restraint to the Lord to save by many or by few." Ah, there is the secret of Jonathan's activity, of his daring, his perseverance, his success: God is on the side of Israel; and, though king and father may have transgressed, and priest and people tremble and melt away, there is One who needs no great armies to make the victory sure; One who buried Pharaoh with his host in the waters of the sea; One who smote Og, the giant king of Bashan, through all his massive fortresses of stone; One who threw down the walls of Jericho at the blast of the trumpet; One who, with Gideon's little band, chased the countless multitudes of the Midianites; who overwhelmed the Philistines from Mizpeh to Ebenezer by the terror of his thunder. With Him there is no restraint to save by many or by few. And the simple trust of that young man inspires his comrade to do with him, and to dare. Quietly he answers: "Do all that is in thine heart: turn thee; behold, I am with thee according to thy heart."

Then, the soldier's duty settled, the general speaks. But what generalship! Said Jonathan: "Behold, we will pass over unto these men, and we will discover ourselves unto them. If they say thus unto us, Tarry until we come to you; then we will stand still in our place, and will not go up unto them. But if they say thus, Come up unto us; then we will go up; for the Lord hath delivered them into our hand: and this shall be a sign unto us."

One would think that an enemy so confident in their strength as not to take time to reconnoiter, but who should defiantly call, "Come up unto us!" would be a foe worthy of more respect than to be attacked in front. But Jonathan had a Captain whose tactics he had learned. Lacking nothing of power, He feared no odds, and when mere men, deceived by appearance of weakness, boastfully set their strength against it in contrast, then the Lord would smite, and all the world should have to confess that He was mightier than they. That plan and that sign had been given to Jonathan while he stood in silent prayer upon the top of Migron, and now he confidently acted upon them.

So those two young men passed on through the wood and around the base of the hill, and began the steep descent of the path that led to the valley below. At the point where they came down, the broad valley is divided, on the left, by two steep, rocky hills that project from the higher land on the west. The one on the side toward Geba was named, from its pointed shape, Seneh, a thorn. That on the north, toward Michmash, had suggested for itself, by its head of whitish chalky stone gleaming by night or day, the name Bozez, shining. Hidden partly in the shadows of these hills, and partly by the rolling hillocks of the vale, Jonathan and his armor-bearer made their way toward the mile-distant border wall. Not yet had the careless watchers upon the Philistine heights discovered the foe; or, seeing, had but thought them two Hebrew fugitives, skulking for a safer hiding-place.

So these two drew near to the frowning steep. Then, casting aside all stealth and caution, and stepping out upon a high knoll, they stood and measured with their eyes the well-nigh unscalable sides of the precipice before them. From the east, straight through the narrow gorge into which the valley contracted below, the rising sun poured in its shafts, rebounding from the bright armor of the young men. Then from the heights came the hail of a Philistine voice; for the watchers of the garrison had discovered them. But they said among themselves, with scornful laughter, "Behold, the Hebrews come out of the holes where they had hid themselves;" and, leaning over the rock at the brink, the sentries cried, mockingly, "Come up to us, and we will show you a thing."

The response none expected. To Jonathan that

A Man of Valor

mocking call was a message from God; and, turning to his armor-bearer, his face aglow with the light of certain success, he said, in a tone of glad conviction, "Come up after me; for the Lord hath delivered them into the hand of Israel."

The challenge of the Philistine sentries brought no answering voice. The two figures far below, after their momentary disclosure of themselves, seemed to make haste to be hidden again. They plunged forward under the brow of the precipice, and were lost to view. The watchers upon the summit sank back again at ease, with no thought of possible danger from that short episode. Many were the Hebrews already in their camp, meek-browed and shrinking; if two more should choose to come, perhaps they might slink in among their fellows, if they chose; why should a Philistine take notice? If they were indeed no deserters, but merely stragglers, perchance even scouts, it was of little moment to the conquerors: they were well entrenched; they knew the pitiful state of their despicable enemy, and need take no alarm at that distant inspection.

Little did they think that their scornful challenge had been accepted; that down below, toiling up a hidden path, came on a force that threatened assault, that trusted in invincible power, that expected complete victory. Yet even so! The power of the Hebrew army, the might of the God of battles in those two men of faith, was assailing the Philistine host.

Clinging to vines and shrubs that grew in the crevices of the rock, breasting the steepest places, and pulling, pushing themselves onward, upward, by hands and feet, Jonathan and his armor-bearer stormed the heights of Michmash. Was ever there sight so strange? Two lone men were taking by escalade an impregnable fortress, under the very feet of a challenging foe!

Had they seen them, the Philistine soldiers could but have regarded them with astonishment, wondering at what desperate need could send them up that perilous height. Mere stragglers, fugitives, they must have counted them; and when they should reach the top, they would do with them as the whim of the moment might direct,— clap them upon the back in admiration for their wonderful climb, thrust them headlong again to the place whence they came, save them to join their craven comrades who had already enlisted in the Philistine service, or bind them as captives to toil in the mills of Ekron. But they saw them not, and in fancy of perfect security they lolled idly upon the grassy brink.

A Man of Valor

Slowly the toiling forms draw toward the top, Jonathan ahead, his armor-bearer following him. With one last wrench, one final leap, the agile prince stands upon the summit, and the amazed sentries fall back with gasps of astonishment. The sun borrows fiery gleams from his shining mail, and flings them into their faces; his eyes are flaming with the glory of the Lord of hosts. His hand seeks his sword at his side, and now he smites. Astonishment, fear, consternation, seize his nearest foes. Instead of captors, they are cravens. What does this vision of might and power and glory portend? Is it really war? Will this Hebrew fight? The question is answered by the sweep of the gleaming sword: one and another and another fall before his avenging arm. And now his armor-bearer leaps up behind him, and joins him in the mighty battle-shout, "Jehovah-nissi! The Lord our banner!"

Upon the space of half an acre the one-sided battle is waged, and the lightning strokes of the army of God have stricken down all that careless group that watched the ascent. But the commotion extends, the panic spreads. The fear of the Lord has fallen upon the garrison. They have been attacked at their strongest post, and the heights are taken! The host is assailed in flank and rear! Dagon has forsaken them, and fights no more! In consternation the mighty thousands turn to escape. They trample one another; they fight for room to flee; their terror-stricken eyes behold foes in friends.

It was no mere senseless fear that fell upon them. The presence of the great God was there; the earth itself quaked; and every one knew that destruction was determined upon them. The powerful horses, harnessed to the great war-chariots for a speedy expedition, now, stampeded by the terror that everywhere prevailed, broke through the ranks, mowing and crushing their way through all the multitudes of them that were their masters. The host melted away, and went on beating down one another.

Back upon the hill of Migron, the awakened camp had its attention called to the distant garrison upon Michmash. An unusual commotion seemed to be going on in the Philistine camp. Did it mean the beginning of the onward sweep of Israel's enemies? Was the tide of battle about to roll around the devoted little band upon Migron? — No; there was no advance: the host melted away, and rolled back from the face of Michmash.

The keen mind of Saul went immediately to

A Man of Valor

the cause. Though guessing the secret, he called for his band to marshal in rank, and the roll-call was taken. Every number was answered but those of Jonathan and his armor-bearer. Then Saul sought to have word from the Lord, and he called to the priest, Ahimelech, that he might be told through him of what was done, and what he should do. But while he talked with the priest, the commotion in the distant camp increased, and the noise of the struggle came faintly, but ever more strongly, to the ears of the eager soldiers, and even to Saul's distracted senses, until, impatient of further delay, and reckoning action the greatest virtue then, he cried to the priest, "Withdraw thine hand!" and, forming his ranks, he rushed with them toward the battle-ground.

When his breathless band had gained the field, they found the battle won for them. The Philistines were fighting, struggling, crying in terror and death. Plunging into the dust, the little company hewed down their enemies, never pausing except when they came to those Hebrew deserters who had joined themselves to the Philistine host. These, relieved of their fear, and ready to smite with their own people when victory seemed certain, turned upon their recent fellows the arms with which they had been furnished;

and the army of Israel swelled into thousands. Then, as the battle rolled on, from the caves and the thickets and the strongholds poured out the fugitive men of Israel, and joined themselves to the jubilant forces of the victors.

But it was not the host that gained that battle. No captains of fifties nor captains of thousands could boast of the terrible defeat they had inflicted upon their enemies that day. The Captain of the Lord's host was there, and by lightning-flash and thunder-stroke and quakings of the earth he fought to make known his might among the heathen; for one young man had trusted in him and permitted him to work.

So north and west the harried host rolled toward the descent of Beth-horon. Amid rout and ruin, blood and death, the shame of Israel was wiped out in the disastrous overthrow of their pitiless enemy. Philistia bowed low from the heights of Michmash; and never again could she raise her head so high above the people of the Lord.

CHAPTER III

Honey and Blood

THE day that saw the terrible overthrow of the Philistines seemed by the voice of God in all the arts of nature, to be speaking the glory and the joy of Israel — a bright and beautiful day of Zif, " the month of splendor,"— the resurrection time of the year.

This incursion of the Philistines had begun in the usual early foray which they made when the first of the fruits of the land were about to ripen, or when the harvest was in progress; and the present increase in numbers of their army had been occasioned only by the defeat of their garrison at Geba, and their consequent determination to crush the audacious prince who had accomplished it.

It was now the time for the barley harvest, but over all the green and golden uplands of Mount Ephraim the terror of the Philistine name had chased the people away from their homes to hide in the coverts of the rocks; and, save where the Philistines had robbed or trampled them, the fair fields of grain were everywhere ready to drop their precious burden before it could be gathered. The land of Benjamin in those days held perhaps fewer inhabitants than any other equal area in all Israel, except the desert lands of Simeon and lower Judah; for Benjamin had been but a few generations before almost exterminated, and was now one of the smallest of the tribes. Yet the territory was by no means thinly populated. In its longest part not more than twenty miles, and in its widest scarce fifteen, yet it, some twenty years after this time,[1] could furnish to the newly-crowned David over three thousand men-at-arms, while "the greatest part of them kept the ward of the house of Saul." The country was hilly, and some of it, as at Michmash, rocky and sterile, but the most of it was, under cultivation, fair indeed. The steepest hills, upon the top of which, for greater security, were most often built the walled towns, were terraced and planted to vineyards and orchards. Here and there might be seen a flat-roofed cottage, perched upon a slope or nestled in a hollow of the hills, its white walls of lime-washed stone contrasting pleasantly with the gray and green of the olive, the pomegranate, the fig, the grape, and all the beautiful fruits of that pleasant land. The hillsides and fields where the flocks

---

[1] See Note 1, Appendix.

and herds pastured were brilliant with rose-hued anemones and beautiful lilies-of-the-valley, while the fragrance of the later-blooming grapes was wafted by every passing breeze.

The borders of the road that led from the Jordan valley through the lands of Benjamin and Ephraim, toward the Philistine plain, winding around the hills and plunging through the gorges of this mountain land were verdant and smiling under the early rains, and all the country seemed happy and prosperous. Yet the flocks were scattered upon the hills with none to keep them; the few kine that lingered around the homesteads lowed plaintively through the bars, or with secret satisfaction welcomed the liberated calves that had been taken from them. An air of solitude and desolation hovered around the deserted houses; for all the households had forsaken their homes in the fear that everywhere lived of the extortion and cruelty of the lords of Gath and Ekron. So the morning sunlight revealed no stir; the seaward breeze bore no sound of human activity; and only the woods and caves could tell of furtive forms that watched from their coverts for the dread sight of the expected spoilers.

The creatures of the wood and field ventured

out to inspect the domain of man. The little hares were trespassing upon the gardens, and kept careful watch for only their four-footed enemies. A lion from the distant ravine, belated but fearless, stalked the frightened flock. Across the dusty road there trotted two little foxes, and, entering the vineyard that bordered the wayside, chewed at the vine-stalks of the tenderer plants. The far-away call of the turtle-dove, inexpressibly mournful in the solitude, punctuated the deep silence of the heavens.

Bees were winging their musical way from flower to store and store to flower, eagerly gathering the abundant harvest with which their garners already overflowed. Just where our eye would rest upon it, near Beeroth, the road swept abruptly around a projecting spur of the Ephraimic range, a spur that was crowned with a noble growth of oak. Here, if the eye might have followed them, could the swarms of nectar-laden bees have been seen winging their heavy flight. Tree after tree there held store of honey so abundant that from many an opening it dripped upon the rocks below, and even upon the low branches of the trees, here and there, might be found the laden comb, which those tireless workers had found it impossible to crowd within. So, in the

A Man of Valor

glowing light, droned on the heavy morning to an unhappy people.

Yet not many points had the finger of the garden dial cast, when to the ears of the hidden, hunted watchers upon the wooded heights was borne the sound of distant tumult. Eyes were strained toward the east, from which the breeze brought evidence of conflict, and the heart of every trembler beat faster with the hope, which he scarcely dared to entertain, that this meant help for Israel. Rising or sinking with the fitful wind, the noise yet swelled to greater and greater volume, and the impression became a certainty that a great battle was in progress; that it had become a rout; that the course of the combatants rolled this way.

An hour passed, while the clouds of dust and the roar of a disorganized host came nearer and nearer. The wild-eyed flocks huddled together in consternation; the jackals slunk away over the hills; and the soaring eagle whistled and screamed as his eye pierced the distance, and discerned what man could not behold.

Then, bursting through the defiles of the closer hills, swept, weaponless and disheveled, a little body of horsemen, faces blanched and eyes wide-staring, urging their way to hoped-for safety on the distant plain. Rout and riot followed in their wake. Chariots and horsemen, the steeds free-reined and ungovernable, choked the narrow path, overturning and overthrowing warrior and horse, as the rabble pressed and fought. Where the road took its sudden turn, there piled up around the first mishap a chaos of wreckage and frenzy, beasts crazed and men turned demons, while behind them pressed still the mass of fugitives from the terror-stricken field of Michmash.

Down through the mob of lesser men strode a band of warriors of gigantic stature, roaring and cursing in sheer fright. Ill fared the Philistine warriors then that impeded the course of these their lords of Gath. Backed against the obstructing heap that filled the road, mailed forms turned desperately upon those who followed them, and fought in despair to save their lives from the hands of those who had been their comrades. Shriek and curse, impotent prayer and unheeded command, rent the air, while the terrible army of the enemies of God destroyed itself.

Then from the rear, adding terror to terror, came another cry, clear and trumpet-like above the hoarse roar of the rabble, the resounding battle-cry of the victors, "The sword of the Lord and of Saul!" And a little, compact band of

A Man of Valor

Israelite warriors clove through the massed ranks of the Philistines, dealing the blows of the One whom they named and whose strength nerved their arms. At their head was seen the familiar visage of him we watched from Migron to Michmash. Now his face, though covered with the grime of battle and sagged with the terrible fatigue of the morning's fight and pursuit, was lightened with the glory that came down from heaven to win the field.

Renewed terror spurred the fugitive ranks once more against that barrier of dead men and beasts and broken vehicles. The rush of the rear forced hundreds under, and a horrible, gory incline was laid over the ridge upon the bodies of writhing men. Over this poured the hunted hundreds that yet held lease of life. The Hebrews, viewing the ghastly spectacle just before them, paused, and then, led by their young captain, essayed to climb the step sides of the hill around which the road wound, knowing that they would find upon the other side still better opportunity to smite the fleeing enemy, of whose army this was only a fragment.

As they climbed the sheer ascent, and breathless and exhausted crept into the cool shade of the wood that crowned its summit, the welcome sight of dripping honey met their eyes, famished and exhausted as they were, as a gift from heaven. He who reached it first, with the staff of his spear dipped a portion of a honey-comb and began to eat. But not one who came after him followed his example. They looked disapprovingly and even with horror upon their young lord, and one of them, putting out a restraining hand, declared to Jonathan, "Thy father straitly charged the people with an oath, saying, Cursed be the man that eateth food this day," "that I may be avenged on mine enemies."

This was an oath that Saul had hastily exacted of his men, when, after their arrival at Michmash, he had seen the possibilities of the defeat then being inflicted upon the Philistines. Anxious to secure the fullest fruits of the coming victory, he determined to prevent the delay and loss that would come from the people's stopping to eat. Capable himself of enduring the greatest fatigue, he would ask his people to follow his example, and lose no moment the work of which would add to the victory. If this day should see the utter breaking of the power of these haughty heathen, he could see reflected upon himself a glory which never before could be claimed by any in Israel, nor even in Tyre or Egypt. Yet

A Man of Valor

his judgment, warped by the gloomy brooding of the past few days, and unguided by the Spirit of God, was faulty in its exercise at this crisis. By requiring of the people what only his own iron frame could stand, he sowed the seeds which should reap a speedy harvest, not only of physical distress to his men, but of transgression against the laws of God.

And this Jonathan saw. It was no spirit of self-justification nor an unfilial thought that prompted him to make the reply: "My father hath troubled the land: see, I pray you, how mine eyes have been enlightened [my fatigue overcome], because I tasted a little of this honey. How much more, if haply the people had eaten freely to-day of the spoil of their enemies which they found? — for had there not been now a much greater slaughter among the Philistines?" The spoil of the Philistines strewed every road and all the fields by which they fled. Stores of food were abandoned, as well as raiment and costly articles of furniture and jewelry that their flight impelled them to cast away. The men of Israel were very faint, and their pursuit lagged; yet, because of the oath, no man dared touch anything he might see; for the word of the oath had passed from mouth to mouth as the men of Israel joined the ranks of the six hundred. But Jonathan, far in advance, and buried in strife, had received no intimation of it until after he had transgressed. And then, fearless before wrong judgment of even the king, as he was unafraid in the presence of his enemies, he spoke true judgment where it had been warped.

Over upon another road that led toward the plain, the towering form of King Saul, terrible in his aroused battle-ire, led the swelling force of Israel in its onslaughts upon the fleeing enemy. Everywhere the woods and the hills swarmed out their hundreds, who, arming themselves with the cast-away weapons of the Philistines, flew, confident of victory, upon their foes. The battle swept on, mile after mile adding to the disaster and loss of the fleeing army, until, as night approached, the city of Ajalon, in the Philistine plain, raised its pitying walls to shelter a part of that poor remnant of a once proud host, while many hundreds of the rest still fled on toward their homes.

Stopped partly by the forbidding walls of the city, and, indeed, incapable, because of exhaustion, of a farther pursuit, the famished men of Israel, knowing the oath of Saul now to have been kept to the end, could restrain themselves no

A Man of Valor

longer. Falling upon the cattle and sheep they had taken as spoil, each man slew for himself; and, not waiting for proper cooking, or even to drain the life-blood from the still warm flesh, they began a feast as bloody as had been their battle-scene. The revolting character of the meal can scarcely be imagined. Scattering themselves upon the plain, chasing, seizing, and slaying the frightened animals, with reeking knives they sliced their food from quivering shanks and palpitating sides; and, half roasting the bloody flesh, or in their terrible hunger even leaving it raw, they gorged themselves like wild beasts.

It was not only the physical repugnance which such a feast would arouse, it was the transgression of a direct command of Jehovah involving a principle of holy religion, that made this action a heinous crime. God had told Israel through Moses that the blood was never to be eaten with the flesh. Before the flesh might be eaten, it must be fully drained of that red life-fluid. For said the Lord, " The life of the flesh is in the blood: and I have given it to you upon the altar to make an atonement for your souls; for it is the blood that maketh an atonement for the soul."

In the service of ceremonies which God gave the children of Israel, every part was a type,

an object-lesson, to teach the Israelite some of
the truths of the plan of salvation through the
coming Christ. The offerings made every day
by the priest — the taking of the life of an innocent dove or lamb or bullock, upon which the sins
committed by the person were pardoned — each
pointed forward to the sacrifice which a divine
Saviour was to make in dying that the sins of
all men might be forgiven. The blood of the
sacrifice was touched upon the altar where the
offering was burned, and poured out at its base,
typifying the pouring out of the blood of Christ
upon the earth, where he was offered for our sins.
Thus the blood had a sacred significance, connected with the deepest mysteries of redemption,
and its use for this reason especially, as well as
for reasons of health, was absolutely forbidden
to the people.

Now, unable to restrain their passionate appe-
tite, the people lost all power of control, and
rushed deep into sin against the God who had
wrought so wondrously for them that day. Had
it not been for the foolish oath of the king, they
would not have been brought to this state; and
thus was seen the justice, as well as the mildness,
of Jonathan's declaration, "My father hath
troubled Israel this day."

A Man of Valor

To Saul, still superintending the field, to see that none should escape who could be taken, was brought the word, "Behold, the people sin against Jehovah, in that they eat with the blood." Instantly recognizing the seriousness of the offense, the king answered, "Ye have transgressed: roll a great stone unto me this day." Then his commands were sent out among all the people, that every man should bring his ox or his sheep there to Saul, and slay it upon the great stone, that its blood might be allowed to escape; then he might prepare it and eat. The authority of the king was powerful enough to stop that scene of riot, even when it had proceeded so far, and at the summons the people obeyed, and their hunger was appeased in a more proper manner.

Yet the lesson remains to be learned. Forbidden, by the foolish and glory-seeking vow of the king, to partake of the natural food which God had meant for man,— the fruits and the grain along the road and the honey that came from the flowers of the field,— they were thrown out upon the trodden and fruitless plains of Ajalon, and there, almost starved, were forced to fall back upon the second-rate food of flesh, and even that their hunger drove them to take in a sinful and revolting manner. The man who knows himself to have no close connection with God will always make blunders and cause great trouble when he uses his judgment in the carrying on of the work of God. King Saul is not a lone exception.

Still Saul was anxious to make the victory yet more terrible, and he proposed to his men that they follow the flying forces of the Philistines through all the night, and smite them until not a man of that once vast host should be left. Exultant and loyal, the Hebrew soldiers replied, with hearty shouts, " Do whatsoever seemeth good unto thee." The last rays of the sun were fading from off the hills behind them, and Saul, supported so heartily by his men, hastened the marshaling of his forces for the rapid forward movement which he hoped would be the death-blow to this haughty heathen nation. Trained though he was, like every good Israelite, in the devotional practises of his people, he had now no intention of stopping the practical business in hand for a season of seeking God. And we can imagine that it was almost with impatience that he received the word of the good priest, who had followed all the way with the army, " Let us draw near hither unto God." Nevertheless, acquiescing, he stayed his preparations while Ahimelech prayed. Then

A Man of Valor

through the priest Saul asked of God, "Shall I go down after the Philistines? Wilt thou deliver them into the hand of Israel?" But to that anxious, almost impatient, question there came no answer from the Lord. Saul, grieved and angry that the course of the victory had been stopped, but not daring to proceed without divine approbation, determined to find what was the cause of the Lord's displeasure, that he would not answer when the cause of Israel was in question.

Calling together all the chiefs of the people, he said to them, "Draw ye near hither; and know and see wherein this sin hath been this day. For, as the Lord liveth, which saveth Israel, though it be in Jonathan my son, he shall surely die." There were those present who knew of the unwitting transgression of Jonathan that day, and they trembled when they saw the doom coming. For an oath was sacred. It was no light thing to swear by the throne of the infinite God that anything should be or should not be done. Its solemnity is revealed by Jesus when he tells us, in view of the dread weight of an oath by the name of God or anything in connection therewith, never to swear at all. The most solemn events only, in time and eternity, are thought by God to warrant his making an oath by his own name. Thus, his promise to his people of salvation and a life in Eden restored, he confirmed by an oath. Heb. 6:17. And when, in the closing days of earth, God would hasten the progress of his cause and his coming, a mighty angel swears " by Him that liveth forever and ever, who created heaven, and the things that therein are, and the earth, and the things that therein are, and the sea, and the things which are therein," that there shall be delay no longer. Thus when a man, by the name of the great God, would swear upon even so trivial a matter as this, no one dared transgress that sacredly sealed oath; and God himself respected it, and held those bound by it to its conditions.

Complete silence met the declaration of the king; not a man answered him a word. Awed and quiet, they gathered before that stern-faced king, and read in his countenance the doom of death to him whom the Lord should declare guilty. The lot was another sacred form. By it was made known from the Lord choices to be made for any of his purposes, or the discovery of any secret thing. Just what form the ceremony took we do not know, but it probably consisted of placing in a receptacle pieces of wood or parchment, to the number of those who should participate, one of which pieces would be peculiarly marked. Then

A Man of Valor 51

each man, with eyes closed or averted, would draw from the box one of the pieces; and he who drew the marked piece was "taken by lot." Only by the controlling power of God, of course, could this be accounted certain conviction; and therefore the use of the lot became a most solemn act, consecrated by prayer to God to make it sure.

Saul, energetic and decisive, and determined to fix the guilt within the shortest time possible, commanded that only two lots should be prepared, and directed that all the people should stand upon one side, while he and Jonathan, representing the house of Saul, would stand upon the other. The Lord should say whether the people or the king's house were guilty. Then, in business-like haste, and apparently with little reverence, he uttered the short petition to the Lord God of Israel, "Give a perfect lot." A captain from the other side stepped forth and drew, Saul upon his side also advancing and drawing. The lot fell upon him and Jonathan.

Only one more trial, and the judgment would be given. Through the tense strain of the ordeal the stern voice of the king broke strangely, "Cast lots between me and Jonathan my son." The father and the son faced each other, the one stern as an executioner, form erect, brows bent, eyes set; the other, his noble features, strangely enough, approaching most nearly in this moment of intensity a resemblance to those of his sire, braced by native fortitude and courage born of conscious righteousness. One of the two would be taken, and, according to the decree of the king, must die. Little had Saul supposed, as he emphasized his decision those few moments ago by the declaration, "As the Lord liveth, which saveth Israel, though it be in Jonathan my son, he shall surely die," that there would be opportunity to test that oath.

God must decide between these two. And as the people waited, some among them knowing of the breaking of that morning's oath and seeing the trouble which its hasty utterance had brought upon Israel, did there not come to their minds the question, Will not the just God by the lot throw the responsibility upon the father, and not upon the son? Must he die by whose hand all this victory has been wrought? The two actors in the tragedy stepped forward and drew, and in the dreadful silence the voice of the priest declared, " The lot hath fallen upon Jonathan."

Captain and warrior stood with bated breath to see the end. King over subject, judge against culprit, father for son: what sentiment would be

A Man of Valor

most powerful in the breast of that strong-willed yet passionately affectionate man? Then Saul, vainly casting about in his mind for a road of escape, said, "Tell me what thou hast done." And Jonathan,— no appeal for mercy, no plea that he did not know of the oath, no passionate censure of the foolish charge, came from the lips of that young hero. The day had begun with hope and courage for him; it had progressed with assurance of victory; it had sped in exultant joy of deliverance; and now it was to end in death. But as bravely as he had met the foe, with equal nobility and courage he stood face to face with ignominious death; and he answered, simply: "I did certainly taste a little honey with the end of the rod that was in mine hand, and, lo, I must die."

What could the king reply? His eyes left the face of his son, and rested upon the people who had heard his oath. Forms were bent toward him in rigid suspense; eyes were fixed upon him with an intensity that could not be described; ears strained for the sentence. Had he been alone, Saul might have wavered from the fulfilment of his oath, which would take from him this son, whom his proud and reserved soul held almost as an idol. But his oath had gone out before his army; the word of the king should be kept, that his authority might be respected and his justice feared. Again he fixed his eyes upon Jonathan, and in stern yet grief-filled tones he spoke the sentence, with the familiar but fearful oath: "God do so and more also [if it be otherwise]: for thou shalt surely die, Jonathan."

As when that northern sea of Chinnereth, lying placid and calm beneath the lowering sky that precedes the storm, is suddenly lashed to fury by the tempestuous winds that swoop down upon it over the hills of Naphtali; so over the terrible calm of that twilight judgment-scene there swept, as the words of doom were pronounced, the wrath of a free people, who counted their king their servant. Men sprang forward, half drawing their bloody blades afresh from the sheaths, and between the judge and the condemned there came the living barrier of determined men. Voices rose in earnest expostulation and declaration: "Shall Jonathan die, who hath wrought this great salvation in Israel? God forbid! God forbid! As the Lord liveth, there shall not one hair of his head fall to the ground; for he hath wrought with God this day."

Saul, surprised and overwhelmed by this sudden demonstration of the love and gratitude borne

Voices rose in earnest expostulation

A Man of Valor

toward his son, felt, even in his gratefulness for the salvation so strangely brought both to Jonathan and himself, that his dignity and authority, which he had meant to uphold before Israel by this sacrifice of his paternal love, had been cast down and trampled upon; felt chagrined and humiliated that his judgment of the temper of his people had been so faulty; felt that the affection of the people which he once had held had been transferred to another; and in gloomy state he turned away, and the dark spirit settled again upon his mind. No more thought of chasing the fugitive Philistines! The glory of the day had faded for him; the victory, in the grasp of his unrest and gloom, held little meaning; and with a bitter heart he fought within himself that night a more terrible battle than the day had seen.

With the morning light, silent and grim, he marshaled the armies of Israel and "went up from following the Philistines; and the Philistines went to their own place." The danger to the kingdom had been averted and changed into safety and honor, but he to whom we might expect it would have brought the greatest satisfaction returned, feeling himself a defeated and rejected man.

But over all the land, as the thousands of Israel

dispersed to their homes, were sung the prowess and the nobility of the young Prince Jonathan, and even already some Israelite heart might mutter to itself, "May the day soon come when he shall succeed to the throne!"

CHAPTER IV

The Beginning of Evil

As the traveler, going northward from Jerusalem, passes over the low summit of Mount Scopus, he sees before him a narrow and irregular valley, winding its way among the gray hills straight to the north. Green and beautiful even now it appears, when the late rains have wakened it to life; and though the stony hills, with their outcroppings of gray rock, show little that is pleasing to the eye, the time once was when their slopes, as well as their summits, were verdant with noble forest trees, with vineyards, olive groves, and pastures. Orchards, fields, and vineyards were stone-fenced by the patient toil of the people, and freely over the hills and through the valley ranged the herds of cattle, sheep, and asses.

The watch-towers in the middle of the gardens reared sturdy heads above their wards, and here and there a solitary homestead might be seen standing amid the trees; but for the most part the husbandmen and the shepherds had their dwellings in the town, from whose opening gates they went out each morning to their work, and returned with the setting sun.

Four miles from Jebus (now Jerusalem), we come to a steep hill upon the right side, a hill whose more gradual slope in its lower part is crowned in front by a precipitous cliff. Upon its top, in the days of which we are thinking, stood a town of no mean size, strongly fortified and noble-looking on its lofty seat. This was Gibeah of Benjamin, noted in its earlier history as the town whose evil-doing drew out the wrath of all Israel upon Benjamin, and led to the almost utter extermination of that tribe. It was now in repute in Israel as the home of Saul the king.

Here he had been born, and here his early training had been received. Strong-limbed and active as a boy, he had been the leader of his companions in many a venturesome deed. Though not by birth of the first rank in his own tribe (for his father Kish was but the third son of the chief elder of Gibeah), his daring and enterprise early won him recognition as a leader among his companions. First in every hazardous feat, swiftest of foot, most dexterous of wrestlers, most skilful among those famous right-and-left-handed slingers, he led his young Hebrew comrades in every trial of strength and endurance.

He had climbed to the eagle's eyrie; he had sought out the lion's lair; he had chased the

A Man of Valor

swift desert wolves back to their wilderness. The wild and untameable were his delight, and something of their savagery sank into his own nature. A knowledge of his superiority begot and nourished in him a greater self-confidence; the consciousness of power within himself inspired him to attempt the accomplishment of whatever task confronted him, with the determination to conquer or to solve in his own might. Yet in many respects his character was noble: frank, openhearted, generous, faithful, he was a lad whom every one might love. But his overweening confidence in himself led him to show a masterful, even tyrannical spirit, begot in him a love of praise and an easily wounded pride, and sowed the seeds of boasting, deception, anger, and revenge. Disdaining to seek the help of others in what he thought himself able to do, he was unused to seeking the help of God in struggles which he could not win, and either fought his daily temptations with desperate if useless valor, or sank into seasons of discouragement which darkened his soul.

A little way up the valley toward Jebus, upon a western prominence, stood the sacred city of Nob.[2] This had for two generations been inhab-

---
[2] See Note 2, Appendix.

ited by priests of the tribe of Levi. Their children often mingled with those of Gibeah, in play and exercise; for the towns were only half a mile apart. Though all the children of the Israelites were taught by their parents with greater or less zeal, the sons of the Levites, who were the teachers of Israel, received special training; and if the hardy Benjamites were first in physical prowess, the priests' children could yet excel them in song and story. Wonderful tales those little Hebrews told one another, as, seated upon some projecting ledge that overlooked a wide stretch of country, they pointed out the places where many of the deeds which they recounted had taken place. Through this valley below them had often passed their great ancestor Abraham, with his countless thousands of flocks and herds and the hundreds of his household; from yonder city of Jebus-salem had come out to meet him the mighty prince and priest, Melchizedek, after Abraham's victory over the Elamite king. Across the distant Jordan might be seen the site of awful Peniel, where Jacob wrestled with his God. The barren plains upon the border of the great Dead Sea showed where, long ago, fair Sodom and her sister cities had reveled and sinned and perished. To the west the plains of Philistia brought memories

Wonderful tales those little Hebrews told

A Man of Valor

of Isaac, of Samson, and of the smiting of the Philistine Ajalon by the fierce Benjamites under Beriah and Shema. And then the story that brought dark looks to the faces of the little Benjamites,— Gibeah's inhospitality and wickedness, when once a Levite tarried there, and the terrible evil that befell its people in consequence. Oh, many were the tales that the Levite children told!

Songs rang over the rolling uplands and through the rocky valleys, songs of triumph and of pleading, memories from the Red Sea, from Sinai, from Tabor, and from Gilead, with more than one plaintive melody that had been born in the heart of some young Benjamite mother,— maiden torn from Jabesh-Gilead or stolen from Shiloh.

Ahimelech, son of the high priest in Nob, and Saul of Gibeah, were the two prominent figures in those boyish gatherings. The mild and sweet-tempered young Levite had yet a will of his own, and the imperious boy of Gibeah could not always receive without passion the steady resistance of that calm will to his own projects. Nevertheless, there was good comradeship between them, and many a time were the two in company, vying with friendly rivalry in trying feats of strength and endurance. Perhaps the influence of those early days in the company of the priests' children had no small effect upon the headstrong Saul in later days; but those influences were outside of his nature, and lasted too short a time.

In his home he was carefully trained in precepts of courtesy and obedience, and to a strict keeping of the law. He was used to the forms and ceremonies of the Jewish religion. He dutifully listened to the reading of Moses' books, and when the law was repeated, he joined with his people in the required, "Amen." At the feasts he saw his father lay his hands upon the head of the lamb, and confess the sins of himself and his family. On Passover night he stood, girded and shod, with his father's family, in the dimly lighted room, and ate the hasty meal of the paschal supper. And in the scanty service of the tabernacle during that troublous time, he stood with the few who attended, perhaps upon the awesome Day of Atonement, when the high priest went into the presence of the living God, and came forth with the glory shining upon him.

But all these ceremonies, which to the spiritual mind and the consecrated imagination would open volumes for thought and meditation, Saul saw but as forms of worship, the doing of which would insure him the blessings that the law promised. He offered the blood of lambs to wipe away his

A Man of Valor

sins; he brought the tithes and offerings to buy a plentiful harvest and an increase of cattle; he kept the Sabbath according to the plain directions of the law, and believed himself a righteous young man. Self-reliant and self-complacent, he despised the heathen, who, though they had no knowledge to serve Jehovah, yet bore their hateful sway over his people.

As he grew toward manhood, the care of his father's possessions devolved more and more upon him. He was strong to bear burdens and eager to hold responsibilities. Yet his ambition never passed, perhaps, beyond the honor of coming finally to be an elder who should sit in the gate of Gibeah, to judge the cases in law that might have to be decided. Perhaps his irrepressible flow of spirits, his active nature, determined his occupation,— to care for the swifter beasts, the cattle, the asses, and the dromedaries,— a herdsman rather than a meditative shepherd.

Here at Gibeah he was married to Ahinoam the Gracious, daughter of Ahimaaz, and here were born to him his four sons, and probably also both his daughters. Thus as a private citizen he lived secluded until he was forty years old, known, indeed, as far at least as Jerusalem, where some of his kinsmen lived, and honored as a man of wealth, a handsome and a sturdy yeoman. Though unknown to Israel generally, he was yet the very one, when once his person and his surface qualities were revealed, to please them all as their ideal of a ruler. The Lord knew this when he directed Samuel to anoint him king. The people, having departed from the Lord so far as to ask a king, must be led by a careful way. First their demand for a monarch was granted; then they were given the kind of king their hearts were demanding, that through the bitter experience which should follow, they might be brought to accord more nearly with God's desire for them in the selection of the king who should be not only the founder of a great dynasty, but the progenitor of the coming Messiah.

Yet the Lord would work also with this their first king, if it were possible, and he ordered things so that the unimpressionable Saul should at the outset be struck into an unwonted sense of helplessness and dependence upon God. No one in Israel, even among his kinsmen, thought of the son of Kish as a candidate for the royal office. The honor did not come in whispers first, to be received with growing favor, until the ears of the young man should be dinned with the nation's demand, and his soul be given a chance to puff

A Man of Valor

itself on the empty winds of popularity. But the obscure herdsman of Gibeah, coming to the prophet on a private errand, was astounded at the sudden announcement of the honor to be conferred upon him. Dazed with the prospect, and seeing the certain opposition of the powerful tribes of Ephraim and Judah to one who sprang from an insignificant family in the smallest tribe, he answered deprecatingly. This was the most teachable moment of his life, and the prophet, by the inspiration of God, hastened to improve the opportunity. The holy oil of consecration was poured upon his head; he was made to feel that the weight of the kingdom was placed upon him as the Lord's captain; and then he was told of the three incidents which should occur on his homeward journey, significant of his release from private affairs, of his acknowledgment by the people, and of his acceptance and inspiration by God.

As the man Saul turned from Samuel to go on his way, his proud heart was bowed, and well at that moment might his name have been changed, as was that of his later tribesman, to Paul,—"little,"— for then he was little in his own eyes. As he passed the hill of Moriah, at Jebus, there approached him a company of prophets, singing one of their inspired songs; and Saul, whose heart had been in meditation all the way, felt the Spirit of God stir him mightily, and he joined in the sacred psalmody. Those who saw him were astonished at the change, and exclaimed, "Is Saul also among the prophets?" Yes, for the first and only time, in a happy sense, Saul was among the prophets; for God had given him another heart; and that strange spirit of quietness, humility, and patience under insult and neglect, remained with him through all the days of his coronation, his first retirement, and his earlier operations in the field of war. Had his heart been yielded earlier to the guidance of that Spirit when it knocked and knocked at the door, had his childhood and early manhood been under such an influence, the history of his tumultuous reign would have been far different. The pride of position, the lust for glory, the jealousy of other favorites, would have been lost in zeal for God's work and devotion to the interests of his people, while the heart communed with him who inspired prophets and taught kings.

Indeed, the influence of those early days of the kingship seems to have had the most lasting influence upon the character of his oldest son. Jonathan, in nature combining the bravery and enterprise of his father with the gentleness of his

A Man of Valor

mother, and always, it seems from Saul's testimony, a willing disciple of the loving but firm-minded Ahinoam, was deeply affected by the change in his father, when he returned from the meeting with the prophet. The home life was of a different character when Saul and Ahinoam joined in impressing upon their sons the truths that made the Hebrews a chosen people. The lads, not far separated in age, were always delighted companions of that strong man in the field and the desert; but Jonathan had not failed to see, heretofore, the lack in Saul of that deep spirituality which he found in his mother; and now that such a mighty change had come upon his father, he turned toward it with the eagerness with which a growing plant turns to the light.

Here was born in Jonathan that unswerving loyalty to his father which never failed; which, through days of sunshine and years of gloom, beat back ambition, evil counsel, and his own indignant wrongs, until at last he laid down his life for him upon Gilboa. In this happy experience he had seen bright possibilities for the career of Saul; and to that beautiful ideal of noble manhood and kinghood he clung in the darkest hours of his father's disobedience, impenitence, rage, and insanity.

It is at Gilgal that we catch the first glimpse of the coming shadow. His heart lifted up through his recent successes and his growing popularity, Saul had lost much of the controlling power of his Spirit-baptism, and his mind reverted toward its former state. He lost the sense of sacredness in the sacrificial rite, and presumed to take the place of priest for his people. The punishment denounced by Samuel, that his house should not continue on the throne, was severe to a Hebrew father, but seemed conditional and perhaps long to be delayed. Saul, resenting the prophet's words, as if they had come from himself, turned from prophet to priest, as if he would reject the former order and form an alliance with the older of the sacred callings.

Yet Samuel felt no resentment toward Saul. He seems naturally to have loved a strong and energetic type of man, and Saul from the first had appealed to his affections. Yet, in any case, he but reflected the Spirit of God, in still clinging with hope to the man who had thus far shown willingness to do right in most of his ways.

The faith and success of Jonathan at Michmash was a test to Saul. If he had seen in the selection of his young son instead of himself to accomplish that great work, a divine rebuke to his attitude

A Man of Valor

at that time, he might have taken the right road back to favor. But that day reveals him to us in an unpleasant light, as seeking to snatch the laurels all to himself, as willing even to sacrifice the hero of the day to the effect of his own self-seeking, and as chagrined and suspicious at the evident transference of affection from himself to his own son.

Yet the years that followed this were filled with mighty deeds. Seeking by activity to relieve the unrest of his own soul, and hoping by his deeds of valor to win more fully the love of his people, Saul plunged into wars with the enemies of Israel on every side. Across the Jordan he invaded the domain of Moab, and that of Ammon, whom he had already smitten; the Edomites, in their rocky fortresses, felt the weight of his arm; roving bands of Amalekites were cut off by his vengeance; and far to the north the one troublesome nation, the kingdom of Zobah, was taught to respect the power that had arisen in Israel. No conquests were attempted: his wars were campaigns of repulsion or raids of revenge; but he steadily raised the spirit of patriotism in Israel, and gained for himself the name of a great warrior-king. Israel's people, indeed, after their humiliation of a few generations past, might well be proud of their king, ascribing, as they would, all the praise to the power of Saul's arm, and little to the influence of the years of Samuel's teaching, strengthening, training, of the souls that made the present successes possible.

Israel had finally come to be ready to follow Saul wherever the trumpet blew. Now the Lord determined to set them to a duty which in his mercy had long been delayed. It would be at once an execution of his justice and a test to Saul and Israel. The nation of the Amalekites, four hundred years before, while the children of Israel were journeying through the wilderness toward Caanan, had been the most cruel and relentless of their foes. They had cut off the stragglers and the sick, murdering and plundering at every opportunity they could find while hovering around the camps and marching columns. Their reputation as the implacable foes of all that is good had been maintained since that time.

Themselves too divided to do more alone than make swift and destructive raids upon Simeon and southern Judah, they had seized every opportunity to join Israel's foes, and plunder, oppress, and exult with them at the miseries they caused. They had joined the Moabites, the Midianites, and the Ammonites in every raid of importance

A Man of Valor

during the four centuries of Israel's presence in Caanan. Fiendishly cruel, they were at once the most pitiless and the most cowardly of all nations. They tore the babe from the mother's arms, and dashed it to death; they forced the laborer whom they entrapped at his threshing-floor, to carry his grain for them to their encampment, and then slew him at the end of the journey; on the march they left the exhausted slave on the desert path to perish of thirst and heat; and they crowned their mountain of crime with the most blasphemous insolence toward the God whom their father Esau had been taught in Isaac's tent to respect and adore.

God said they must be wiped from off the face of the earth. To this work he now commissioned Saul. "Now go," he said, "and smite Amalek, and utterly destroy all that they have, and spare them not; but slay both man and woman, infant and suckling, ox and sheep, camel and ass."

So the trumpet was blown, and the people were gathered together, a great army, two hundred and ten thousand strong. It speaks not a little for the generalship of Saul that with such a host he was able to approach the Amalekite city where their king then lay with most of his people, so secretly as to take it completely by surprise. No doubt the Lord specially favored him in this, that there might be no excuse for disobedience of his commands.

The battle was but a rout, the Amalekites being able to offer little resistance. Saul smote them from Havilah, where he struck his first blow, to Shur, at the border of Egypt. Doubtless after the first battle he divided his great force into detachments, to pursue the fleeing and scattering bands. But the whole campaign was short, sharp, and decisive, and ended in the almost complete extermination of that impious people.

It was the most brilliant victory the Hebrew king had yet gained; but its effect upon him was evil. The days in that desert land Saul saw as revealing himself covered with glory before his troops; and the nights brought dreams of the musical voices and instruments of the daughters of Israel, as they should come forth from the cities to meet the conquering hero. As in his boyhood days, his success, his honor in the eyes of his admiring comrades, lifted up his heart in pride and self-flattery. He was a conqueror, the equal of Sargon and Thothmes. Should he not have some evidence of his prowess to exhibit to gaping multitudes at home? If the fulfilment of the divine command had deprived him of leading a long procession of captives, might he not at least spare one brilliant trophy of his might? So he reasoned; and when the bloodthirsty voluptuary, King Agag, was delivered into his hands, his desire for a grand triumph back in Israel had little trouble in overcoming his scruples. Instead of at once putting him to death, he kept Agag in chains, and reserved him for exhibition in the land which that murderer had so often desolated.

Saul's example was not lost upon his people. They had been commanded to destroy every vestige of the hated nation, even the cattle, the sheep, the camels, and the asses. But, longing in their own hearts to reserve some of this wealth for their own, they quickly caught at the laxity of their chief in obeying God's commands, and saved many of the flocks and herds for themselves.

The march was taken up toward home. Not as the stern executioners of Jehovah's doom did they come, but as a successful band of marauders, decked with the ornaments of the slain, laden with plunder, with far-stretching droves of lowing cattle and bleating sheep.

Within the borders of Judah they paused at Carmel, where Saul erected and carved for himself a monument recounting his great accomplishment, and, like the records of heathen kings, lauding the doer as a mighty warrior, an irresistible conqueror. Then on they went, passing through the sparsely settled wilderness of Judah into the lands of towns and villages, past Ziph and Hebron, Bethlehem and Jebus, everywhere greeted with gaping wonder or exultant joy, and finally came to rest at the sacred center of Gilgal.

But far different was the spirit of one who came to find them. Samuel had received a message from God, and it bore doom for Saul. "It repenteth me," said the Lord to Samuel, "that I have set up Saul to be king; for he is turned back from following me, and hath not performed my commandments." Then he opened to the prophet's mind his perfect knowledge of the character of the king, and ended with the irrevocable sentence of his final rejection. The message was one of grief to Samuel, and he cried to the Lord all that night for mercy upon the proud-hearted king; for pity for his people Israel, whose leader had gone astray; for strength to do his own duty as revealed by God. There in sorrow and tears he tarried before his God, while in the early morning the hosts of Israel swept on to Gilgal.

When at last, strengthened and determined, Samuel came forth to meet Saul, he was told by the people, awestruck at his stern aspect, that

A Man of Valor

Saul, having erected his monument at Carmel, had now gone down with the army to Gilgal. There the prophet, following, found the king.

At the news of Samuel's coming Saul went forth from his pavilion to meet him. The acclamations of his soldiers were rising all about; the music of the singers, chanting the victory, resounded throughout the camp; the flocks and herds, trophies of the grand victory, gave audible witness to his success; the captive Agag was there further to grace the triumph; and Saul, radiant with what he deemed his greater elevation in the estimation of his people, stepped lightly forth to meet the aged seer.

"Blessed be thou," he exclaimed with a deep obeisance, "Blessed be thou of the Lord: I have performed the commandment of Jehovah." But no blessing was returned. Sternly the prophet asked,— by his question revealing the hollow pretense of the king's profession,—"What meaneth then this bleating of the sheep in mine ears, and the lowing of the oxen which I hear?" Did not that commandment which you *have obeyed* contain the injunction, Slay utterly ox and sheep? But this was a little matter to Saul. He said, "The people spared the best of the sheep and of the oxen, to sacrifice unto the Lord thy God; and the rest we have utterly destroyed." Upon the people be the blame! Yet even they have a very worthy motive — they are going to sacrifice all these to the Lord! Saul, led by his pride into transgression, could first cast blame upon the innocent, and then find excuses further to shield himself. Yet even this excuse was an afterthought, and had the people offered these beasts for sacrifice, they would thereby have saved their own, which made their offense none the smaller.

The king would have continued his evasive recital, but the Spirit that was in the prophet, undeceived and unrelenting, restrained him with subduing force. "Stay," were the solemn words of Samuel, "and I will tell thee what the Lord hath said to me this night." The chill of impending evil struck in upon the king. He could but reply, "Say on." And Samuel said, "When thou wast little in thine own sight, wast thou not made the head of the tribes of Israel, and Jehovah anointed thee king over Israel? And Jehovah sent thee on a journey, and said, Go and utterly destroy the sinners the Amalekites, and fight against them till they be consumed. Wherefore then didst thou not obey the voice of Jehovah, but didst fly upon the spoil, and didst evil in the sight of the Lord?"

A Man of Valor

The stubborn heart of the king, fortified with his consciousness of success and the scarce-hushed acclaims of the people, rose up against this accusation, and, giving the lie to the word of the Lord, he declared, in a rush of impetuous words, "Yea, I *have* obeyed the voice of Jehovah, and have gone the way which Jehovah sent me, and have brought Agag the king of Amalek, and have utterly destroyed the Amalekites. But," he added, ready to retreat where the blow must fall upon others, "the *people* took of the spoil, sheep and oxen, the chief of the things which should have been utterly destroyed, to sacrifice unto Jehovah thy God in Gilgal."

"Hath Jehovah as great delight in burnt-offerings and sacrifices, as in obeying the voice of Jehovah?" demanded the prophet. "Behold, to obey is better than sacrifice, and to hearken than the fat of rams. For rebellion is as the sin of witchcraft, and stubbornness is as iniquity and idolatry. Because thou hast rejected the word of Jehovah, he hath also rejected thee from being king."

It was the final sentence, the unalterable doom, delivered in the presence of the army chiefs and all their men. Saul saw in imagination the effect of that denunciation; he saw his army deserting him; he saw himself thrust back to the life of a herdsman on Gibeah's hills; he saw himself undergoing the unendurable humiliation of having another, pronounced more worthy than himself, ascend the throne made vacant by his removal; and, completely broken in his opposition, he bowed himself before the prophet, exclaiming. " I have sinned; for I have transgressed the commandment of Jehovah, and thy words; because I feared the people, and obeyed their voice. Now therefore, I pray thee, pardon my sin, and turn again with me, that I may worship the Lord."

With a lie still upon his lips, even in his confession, Saul dared to ask the favor of God's prophet, that he might retain his honor and his kingdom. But Samuel said, "I will not return with thee; for thou hast rejected the word of Jehovah, and Jehovah hath rejected thee from being king over Israel." He had no more to say; his woe-laden mission was accomplished. He turned to go away. Then Saul, in an agony of fear, unable to utter a word, reached forth and grasped Samuel's mantel to detain him. But it was torn in his grasp. Samuel turned again, and, seizing upon that ready illustration, he declared, " So Jehovah hath rent the kingdom of

A Man of Valor

Israel from thee this day, and hath given it to a neighbor of thine, that is better than thou. And also the strength of Israel will not lie nor repent; for he is not a man, that he should repent."

It was an awful scene,— the venerable prophet, with the light of inspiration upon his face; the stricken, groveling, white-faced king, almost prone before him; the people rooted to their places in awe and fear. Yet Saul seemed to find comfort in the fact that the prophet had turned once more toward him, and finding his voice, he pleaded again, "I have sinned; yet honor me now, I pray thee, before the elders of my people, and before Israel, and turn again with me, that I may worship Jehovah thy God." Moved with a divine pity, and a clear foresight of the disaster that would follow his refusal, in the disorganization of the army and the complete disheartenment of the people, Samuel consented; and Saul, his soul torn in tumult, yet outwardly calm, stood with Samuel before the multitude, and worshiped the Lord.

The service finished, Samuel, as if taking again the place of chief ruler, demanded that the captive Amalekite be brought before him. The wretch was brought. He was flattering himself that, though in misfortune, he need not expect death. So, clothed in his most sumptuous raiment, his person decked and dazzling with the gorgeous ornaments of the desert-dweller, he came into the presence of Samuel. Bowing himself before the white-haired seer, whose unyielding brow threw again upon him the dread of death, he exclaimed, as if to reassure himself as well as to present his prayer to his judge, "Surely the bitterness of death is past." The reply of Samuel, a death sentence, in few words summed up the life of crime, and pronounced the doom: "As thy sword hath made women childless, so shall thy mother be childless among women." And he hewed him to pieces before the Lord.

The day was closing, the night coming on; and Samuel, toiling over the hills toward Ramah, was beginning the lament for Saul which ended only with his years.

The night came on in Gilgal, and the black shadows of the Judean hills lengthened their chilly arms, and shot pointed fingers at the camp on the plain. An oppressive stillness rested over all the encampment: no martial clang of weapons rang down the aisles; the voice of song, of praise or revelry, was absent; and the low bleating of the flocks upon the plain, which alone seemed to break the terrible calm, came in only as an au-

The day was closing, the night coming on

dible accusation which all nature was silently impressing. No sacrificial fires were kindled, and only here and there a mourner among the warriors dared lift a voice in scarcely whispered prayer. Abner, the king's captain, silently set the guards beyond the camp, and, turning, stalked with set face toward his quarters.

The king no man saw. But in his tent, alone, save for one silent companion, there raved, it seemed, a madman whom no hand could hold. "A better than I! A better than I! Heardest thou that, Jonathan? God hath rent the kingdom from me, even as I shred in my hands this mantle of the accursed Agag. Piece by piece, rag by rag, thread by thread, God shall rend the kingdom from me! Do the people leave? Do they melt away as in that first time here in Gilgal they sneaked to their holes when Samuel came not? And now he comes. Then he cursed me; now he curses me! A better than I! Who is a better than I? Has any smitten Gath and Ekron as I have done? Has any delivered Israel from the scourges of Ammon and Moab? Whom will Dan beyond Naphtali now thank because they rest in security from Damascus? A better than I — Jonathan, is it thou? But no: 'He hath given it to a *neighbor* of thine, who is better than thou!' Will he strike me in that day? Shall I fall by the hand of an Israelite? Jonathan, wilt thou smite? Shall the uncircumcised Philistines strike my head from off my shoulders? And wilt thou strike with them, Jonathan, my son? I reared thee on the hills of Gibeah, and thy strong limbs have paced with mine since thou wast able to leave thy mother's knee; thy hand hath been upon my heart through all these years. Now thou canst never step upon the throne when I shall fall, unless — art thou better than I? A *neighbor,*— who is he? O God! I worshiped thee to-day with Samuel by my side; I offered thee a bullock and a lamb; and all that I have done for thee wilt thou forget? I smote the tyrant Nahash when my sword was young; I have bathed it, ah, how many times, in blood of the Rephaim; and Amalek I have utterly destroyed for thee. Even Agag is dead. Strike not the scepter from my children's hands; yea, not from Jonathan's. Thou knowest he is better than I. And I have taught him how to use the bow, and he can sling — yea, he shall sling Philistia out beyond the western sea; and he shall climb, yea, as he climbed at Michmash for the glory of thy name! Have I not reared him like a gazelle upon the hills? Swifter than the eagle, stronger than the lion

A Man of Valor

of the reedy covert, is my son. Wilt thou not hear, for Jonathan? Jonathan!"

"Father, the night is come, and the watch-fires gleam upon the low-hung clouds like the glory of God when he turned again his face toward Israel, after the sin of our father Aaron. Wilt thou not rest?"

CHAPTER V

The Cleaving of Souls

"Gibeah of Saul" the royal city was now called. Saul had become the most commanding figure on the Syrian coast, and his city gained prominence from his name. Zobah and Phenicia quiet, Philistia restrained, Ammon and Moab subdued, and Amalek destroyed, the Hebrew king might rest, it would seem, in his mountain home, and give his mind fully to the internal development of his kingdom. Samuel's denouncement of his evil course might fade from the minds of men should prosperity seem to wait upon him; for so fickle is the human memory. Few grasp the meaning of the Lord's judgments: many there are to denounce when he rebukes the righteous; and few are there to remember through the lapse of time his warnings to the wicked.

The wide, wide world was opening to the rising Hebrew nation; and eagerly, after the centuries of obscurity, the people of repression reached their timorous hands to plunge into Egypt's coffers and Zidon's marts. The merchantmen of Issachar and the northern tribes, long accustomed to the luxuries of neighboring heathen courts, en-

A Man of Valor

couraged and built up the caravan trade through the valley of Esdraelon, where the routes met from Tyre and Zidon, Damascus, Aram, and Chaldea, and from the land of the Hittites in the North, to enter the great road that lay along the coast through the country of Philistia. Benjamin and Ephraim, too, drank of the flowing caravan stream that wound among the hills of their uplands, and through the Jordan valley, to feed the markets of Moab, Gilead, and Geshur.

From a commonwealth of land-owners and tillers, Israel was fast developing into a nation of traders and travelers. The awakening gave opportunity for the carrying of the true faith to the remotest bounds of the earth; it also opened avenues for the inflow of luxury and corruption, greed and oppression. Which did the change portend?

Again the smith's anvil rang in the valleys, and the flail beat time to the monotonous treading of the oxen at the threshing-floors; the distaff and the loom were converting the products of field and pasture; and the husbandman toiled in security in his fields and vineyards. For were not Saul and Jonathan watching from their craggy heights, to fend off what daring invaders should venture to intrude? From Dan to Beersheba the land sang, in the happy knowledge that Israel was once again free.

Yet one spot there was which did not share in the general joy. At Gibeah the royal palace was in gloom. There was gayety there, and pomp. Princes and princesses gathered around them the beauty and chivalry of Israel, and the affairs of the court were rendered more brilliant by the presence of the women, a liberty, in the Orient, peculiar to Israel. The king's sons, bold and dashing; his daughters, the younger, at least, distinguished for an independence of mind and proud but ofttimes winning manners,— these, with the chiefs of the army, the elders of the council, and the younger men of distinction in war and diplomacy, with their daughters, their sisters, and their wives, formed an assemblage at once imposing and fascinating.

But that bright sun whose shining had seemed to drive the shadows from the remotest parts of Israel, had its eclipses. Across the clear and purposeful policy of the king there struck at times a sinister shadow. The palace held its secrets, of which men in the dark hours spoke guardedly and with foreboding. Yet they alone who were closest to the king knew at all what the evil thing was, and they but vaguely.

A Man of Valor

Since that fearful day at Gilgal, when Saul had heard his doom at the mouth of the prophet Samuel, there came times when his mind would fain have rested from the toils of statecraft, when a horror of darkness clutched his soul in a strangling grasp; and, buffeted and tormented by an evil spirit, he raged like a madman, and ever more wildly as time went on. To what purpose were all his toils, all his successes in field and hall, if at the end they must be wrested from his grasp, and torn from the hands of his son? Israel, indeed, might profit by his labors; but he, his children, and all his house, were doomed to abasement, perhaps to extinction. And this, to the mind of Saul, was a fate too grievous to be borne. He could not comprehend, far less rise to, the self-abnegation of Moses, that earliest leader of this people, when he cried, "O Lord God, destroy not thy people and thine inheritance, which thou hast redeemed through thy greatness. . . . Look not unto the stubbornness of this people, nor to their wickedness, nor to their sin." " Yet now, if thou wilt forgive their sin —; and if not, blot me, I pray thee, out of thy book which thou hast written." To Saul the remembrance of his disgrace wiped out the thought of every benefit which had been bestowed; for he and his sons should not partake of them. He could not see the mercy there was in it to him, nor that if he would accept the doom of the Lord, the Lord would make that very doom the means of his salvation,— a blessing to him and to his son. The purpose of the Lord was hidden to Saul behind the barrier of his own selfishness. And when his mind ceased from the toils of war and statecraft, it was often but to go into paroxysms of insane rage, when he raved of Samuel's injustice, God's ingratitude, Jonathan's misfortune, his own injury, and the haunting terror of that neighbor who was to take his throne.

His attendants, stricken with this dreadful calamity, and helpless before a mind disease so unknown in Israel, could only conceal from the people, as best they might, the worst of the knowledge, and endure in affright the violence of the outbursts.

Upon the prince fell the heaviest of all the ponderous burden. It was Jonathan who must meet the embassies from Zoan, from Tyre, and from Nineveh, that waited in vain for Saul; it was Jonathan who must counsel with the elders from Judah and from Manasseh beyond Jordan; it was Jonathan who must settle the wrongs of the oppressed and intervene in the quarrels of

A Man of Valor

the violent; and it was Jonathan who must bear the wildness of the king's frenzy, for he best could quiet it. No simple ailment was that fever of the brain. No courtier, no damsel nor matron, could calm the tempest by any art of conversation; no priest, be he ever so skilled in the healing art, could drive away that malady.

But at last his servants, made wise by their needs and bold by their extremity, devised and urged upon the king a remedy. "Behold now," they said, "an evil spirit from God troubleth thee. Let one who is a skilful player upon a harp be brought before thee, and when the evil spirit cometh upon thee, he shall play with his hand, and thou shalt be well." The king doubtfully consented, and upon the recommendation of one of the courtiers, there was brought into the presence of the king a young shepherd, David, the son of Jesse of Bethlehem. He was said to be a skilful player upon the harp, and, though so young, was reported already to be heroic in war and prudent in counsel.

Saul was now almost delivered up to the influence of the evil spirit, and upon the weary shoulders of his eldest-born were pressing ever more heavily the affairs of state. Borne down, not by the duties which so unnaturally devolved upon him, but by the secret grief that made him its prey, the once buoyant and courageous prince was sinking into dejection and heaviness of heart. Saul in his lucid hours might assume temporary control, and exhibit his usual energy, but this display of his old-time vigor only made the gloom the greater when he plunged again into the depths of his insanity.

But with the coming of the musician, the shepherd lad from Bethlehem, the cloud began to lift. When the dark spirit came upon the king, the young harper came before him, and played and sang songs of his own composing. The harmony of his performance, and the melody of his voice, wonderful in its power, controlled the madman with the charms of that heavenly spirit which he had lost; and it was not long until the harper was able to sway the emotions and the whole mind of the afflicted king. Day by day and week by week the power of the harper grew, and Saul loved him greatly, so that he made him his armor-bearer. He was almost constantly with the king, and Jonathan, now relieved of that great weight, was more free to conduct judiciously the affairs of the kingdom.

In the presence of the king, and on the few other occasions when he met him, Jonathan looked favorably upon the young man who had wrought this change that gave every promise of being permanent; but the youth as well as the modesty of the son of Jesse limited the interest of the prince, burdened as he was with cares, to little more than formal intercourse.

The shepherd-musician could not be induced to tarry at the court longer than his services were required by the condition of the king; and often, when the malady was allayed, he would return to the quiet of the hills and the folds, only to be recalled when the moodiness of the king threatened a return of his illness.

It was during one of these absences of David from court that the long quiet of peace was broken again by the alarm of war. The Philistines, whose inveterate hostility could not long be concealed, broke the irksome truce, and advanced up the valley of Elah, toward the heart of the Judean territory. Again the war-trump of Saul sounded, and Israel gathered at the call. The valley of Elah is a depression running up from the plain of Philistia among the hills of Judah; in the winter there flowed through it a great torrent; in the summer the deep channel of the river lay rocky and dry. The valley was the natural road from the Philistine cities into the Judean country, and the invaders had the double purpose of plundering the stores of the people and of challenging to battle the Hebrew king.

Roused to action, Saul gathered a force, and, hastening southward, set up his standard on the northern brink of the valley of Elah, at a place called Ephes-dammim, "The staying of bloodshed." The valley here is about a mile wide, except that on the north side, where Saul pitched his camp, five tongues of high land run out nearly to the middle of the valley. On the south side the Philistines pitched their camp, and thus strongly intrenched, each army lay watching the other. Saul was waiting until the fast arriving levies from the more distant tribes should make him strong enough to attack; and the Philistines, on their part, counted the position of the Hebrews too strong to be taken by direct assault.

They had, however, another resource. It was not unusual, in ancient times, and, indeed, in comparatively modern times, for opposing armies to send out single champions, upon the result of whose encounter more or less might depend, according to the agreement of their supporters. There were in the camp of the Philistines, in the contingent from Gath, some of those gigantic warriors, the descendants of the sons of Anak, whom Caleb had, centuries before, expelled from Hebron. Their degeneracy was not less shown by their extraordinary stature (nearly twice that of an ordinary man) than by other marks of their abnormal development. Some members of the family had each an extra toe and an extra finger. Before the conquest of Canaan by the Israelites, they had been a great power in the land. Adonizedec and his four confederates, whom Joshua slew, were of this race.[3] They held great power over the native Canaanites, and were their lords. Joshua expelled them from the mountain fortresses; Caleb drove them from their last stronghold, Hebron; and they became refugees in Gaza, Gath, and Ashdod. Though the Philistines feared and doubtless hated them, yet their power, and, above all, the aid they could give in time of war, won for them a home in the Philistine country, and a foremost place in the ranks.

Now one of these, Goliath by name, was put forward by the Philistines to offer single combat. He was a terrible champion. Ten feet high, and broad in proportion, he wore a brazen coat of mail weighing one hundred seventy-five pounds, besides a heavy brazen helmet and leg-armor. His spear-head alone weighed over twenty pounds.

---
[3] See Note 3, Appendix.

He was girded with a ponderous sword, and his huge shield was carried before him by his armor-bearer. His voice was a bellow like that of the wild bulls of Bashan, and when he walked, the ground trembled with his tread.

Down from the camp of the Philistines, Goliath came into the valley below, and, striding across toward the Israelite camp, he roared his challenge to Israel: "Why are ye come out to set your battle in array? am not I a Philistine, and ye servants to Saul? choose you a man for you, and let him come down to me. If he be able to fight with me, and to kill me, then will we be your servants; but if I prevail against him, and kill him, then shall ye be our servants, and serve us."

Not a voice answered him. The men of Israel, terrified by that awful figure and that challenge, so impossible to meet, crouched low behind their entrenchments. And Goliath, glorying in the terror he inspired, bellowed again, "I defy the armies of Israel this day; give me a man, that we may fight together." A man, indeed, to fight with him! He seemed a foe more worthy being assailed with a catapult than with a sword. A hundred men, a whole company, might perhaps assault him with hope of victory, but who could

A Man of Valor

meet him single-handed? Saul, whose valor all Israel loved to sing,— Saul, who loved deeds of daring as he loved his children,— Saul stood but head and shoulders above the ordinary man, and this monster was ten feet tall. And now, filled with dismay at the thought of so unequal a duel, Saul turned away; he was "greatly afraid."

The giant, finding, as he expected, no reply to his vociferations, turned and stalked back across the valley and into the Philistine camp. But the next morning again he came forth, and roared his defiance to the armies of Israel. And scarcely had the bugles blared their insolent welcome the third day when his hoarse tones were heard, filling all the valley, and resounding against the hills, cursing the God Jehovah, and in insulting terms declaring his powerlessness before the might of Gath. Thus day after day the wearisome scene was enacted, varied only by the changes in coarse invective which the shallow wit of the giant could produce; wearisome, but none the less terrifying, for the unanswerable argument of that mailed tower of flesh and blood backed every boast. Thus for forty days Goliath defied Saul and his armies, neither Philistine nor Israelite daring to move against the other, secure in his intrenched position.

And Jonathan, the hero of Michmash, where was he through all these days of shame? Might not Israel trust in him to meet this crisis, and win as glorious a victory as on that day so long ago when he broke the Philistine power? But the soul of Jonathan was worn by the iron that had clanked so long with its heavy step. The weight of a kingdom's government, the care and dread that his father's malady pressed upon him, the noonday business and the midnight vigil, the toil, the exposure, the prayer,— three years of incessant struggle had wound his life with the coils of death, and the lamp of his faith burned low. Besides, the terms of the dread challenge were of moment not merely to himself, but to all Israel. "If I prevail against him, and kill him," shouted Goliath, "then shall ye be our servants, and serve us." What use, then, to adventure one's life when the almost certain result would be death to the giver and slavery for all his people? Better wait to see what other outcome there might be.

But, though the faith of the prince could not rise to the sublime height that it had when with his armor-bearer he scaled the cliffs of Michmash, yet his prayer went up, more incessant than the smoke of the evening and morning sacrifices which the priest offered day after day in the camp,—

A Man of Valor

his prayer that the Lord would send deliverance, and vindicate his name. Might not this be an occasion for the revelation of him who should govern Israel in righteousness after his father? — a revelation for which Jonathan had waited, not only with resignation, but with hope. What to Jonathan were the pomp and the grandeur of earthly glory, when the worm was gnawing at his heart, and when the glory of God was being openly contemned and put to shame before the world by a heathen Philistine? Those years of evil were not wholly evil to Jonathan: in the purpose of God they had served to subdue and train his bold spirit, through suffering, to bring him to bow more humbly at the feet of his Lord, and through that humility to become the greater conqueror.

But day after day the insistent challenge was wearing into Saul's soul, and driving him almost to the frenzy which the camp usually dispelled. In vain he offered rewards to any one who would go out to fight the terrible foe,— to give gold and land, and even the king's own daughter for wife, and to make his whole family free from all exaction of tax and toll. When the bravest shrank, what one of the men of Israel would throw his life away in the arena below? The people cowered; Saul raged; and in his tent Jonathan prayed.

Again and again the opposing hosts were marshaled by their commanders in battle array, as if to begin the combat that day, but the appearance of Goliath, bellowing forth, "Give me a man, that we may fight together!" changed all the hearts of Israel to water, and they stood in their ranks.

But the fortieth day there was commotion in the camp. The news ran through the army that one had been found to meet the challenger. A youth from the town of Bethlehem had come that morning with a message and food for his soldier brothers. It was at the hour when the Philistine champion was shouting his blasphemous words. As he took his ponderous way across the plain, over the dry, stony watercourse, and approached the hills upon which Saul was encamped, the foremost of the Hebrew battle-line, which had advanced down the slope, turned and fled from before him in consternation, taking refuge behind their earthen banks.

The young Bethlehemite was astonished at the sudden panic, as he heard the bull-like voice of the giant cursing God and crying for vengeance on the cowardly dogs who would not fight him.

A Man of Valor

He felt his heart swell with indignation at the insult, and he inquired of a soldier standing by him what should be done to the man who would kill the Philistine and take away the reproach from Israel. He was told of the rewards that had been offered. His further inquiries and bold demeanor inspired the rumor among the warriors that he would go to fight the Philistine.

Word was quickly carried to Saul, who caused the young man to come before him. All the while the roar of the giant's voice was resounding through the camp, and the heart of the youth was fired by the same spirit which had once inspired Jonathan, to meet and vanquish the mighty blasphemer. Brought before Saul, with manly front he declared at once, "Let no man's heart fail because of *him;* thy servant will go and fight with this Philistine." "Thou art not able to go against this Philistine to fight with him," answered Saul, filled with amazement, yet admiration, at the noble bearing of the young man; "for thou art but a youth, and he a man of war from his youth." Truly, indeed, it seemed that such a stripling could not stand a moment before the terrible giant, and true it would have been if there had not been a greater Power than lay in the arms of the shepherd lad alone. But he knew that other Power, and he had proved it.

Modestly, but with fearlessness ringing in his tones, he sought to inspire in Israel's king, by the narration of a desert conflict, the confidence he himself felt. "Thy servant," he said, "kept his father's sheep, and there came a lion, and a bear, and took a lamb out of the flock; and I went out after him, and smote him, and delivered it out of his mouth; and when he arose against me, I caught him by his beard, and smote him, and slew him. Thy servant slew both the lion and the bear: and this uncircumcised Philistine shall be as one of them, seeing he hath defied the armies of the living God. Jehovah, that delivered me out of the paw of the lion, and out of the paw of the bear, he will deliver me out of the hand of this Philistine."

It was a simple eloquence, born of earnestness of purpose and steady faith. The king could answer not a word against it. Out from his conflict of emotions,— admiration, pity, humility, and a new tenderness born at such devotion,— there came back to him for the moment the long-lost feeling of his early kinghood, and quietly he answered, "Go, and the Lord be with thee."

Then upon the slender form of the youth he commanded his own armor to be put,— the brazen helmet, the coat of mail, and the heavy sword. The young man, thus equipped, started bravely out from the entrenchments; but he had not gone far when he was seen to turn back, and he reentered the camp amid the deepest silence of the relieved but half-contemptuous soldiers; for they thought he had reconsidered his rash enterprise, and had weakened. But such was far from being the thought of the brave-hearted youth. He came back to cast off the armor. "I can not go with these," he said to Saul; "for I have not proved them." And so again, much to the amazement of the army, he set out, armed only with his shepherd's sling and staff, to meet the terrible challenger.

Goliath had retired to his own side of the valley, but as he saw a man issue from the Israelite camp and come down into the valley, he surmised that he was one who had at last been found to take up the oft-repeated defiance; and he strode forward, expecting to meet in combat one of the mightiest warriors of Israel, perhaps Saul himself. For a short space of time the youth, as he descended into the dry bed of the stream, was lost to sight. He stopped there for a moment, to gather some missiles for his sling, and, selecting five smooth stones, he put them into his shepherd's bag, and then sprang forth upon the farther bank of the river-course. Goliath had paused, and was looking around for his antagonist. As the lad came into view upon the bank, the giant stared in amazement at his lithe but slender and unarmed figure. Instead of a man, the king of Israel had in mockery sent him a boy, and he with but a staff, as if to drive away a dog. Was this the kind of jest to play upon Goliath of Gath? They should soon feel his vengeance. And yet the fancied insult sank deep into his coarse mind. "Am I a dog," he roared, "that thou comest to me with staves?" And then he poured upon him all the curses of all his gods. "Come to me," he continued hoarsely, "and I will give thy flesh unto the fowls of the air, and to the beasts of the field."

It did not seem an idle threat; for his lofty stature and huge bulk were terrifying enough, and he was encased in armor so perfect that there seemed no hope of piercing it with spear or sword, much less with a pebble from a sling; while his strength and his weapons no man could reckon with. But the reply came back in a fearless, ringing tone, that was carried clearly to the camps on either side: "Thou comest to me," cried the lad, "with a sword, and with a spear, and with

A Man of Valor

a shield: but I come to thee in the name of Jehovah of hosts, the God of the armies of Israel, whom thou hast defied." And he continued, with the certain note of triumph in his voice, "This day will Jehovah deliver thee into mine hand; and I will smite thee, and take thine head from thee; and I will give the carcasses of the host of the Philistines this day unto the fowls of the air, and to the wild beasts of the earth; that all the earth may know that there is a God in Israel. And all this assembly shall know that Jehovah saveth not with sword and spear; for the battle is Jehovah's, and he will give you into our hands."

It was the same faith speaking which had presaged the overthrow of the Philistines at Michmash, only now with a more exultant ring, that well befitted the arena where watching hosts, seen and unseen, were marshaled to behold the conflict.

The giant was enraged. He would cut short this high-toned boasting by such a stripling. So, too mad with fury and contempt to protect himself, he plunged forward toward his foe, pushing back, as if for clearer sight, the helmet that protected his brow. As he rushed across the plain, the light-footed shepherd boy ran forward to meet him, until only a few rods separated them. Then, taking a stone from the bag, he fitted it to his sling, and, poising with the light grace of a practised slinger, he swung it three times around his head, and then, with all the strength of his sinewy young arm, launched it at the giant. His aim was directed, his arm was nerved, by an unseen power. Straight to its mark whizzed the deadly missile, and struck where the raised helmet had left the forehead unprotected. The mighty form shuddered, tottered, threw out its arms, and crashed to the ground.

The camps upon the hills, silent and breathless until now, rose as one man at the astounding outcome. Few, if any, had looked for the success of the Israelite champion; but now, as he sprang forward upon the prostrate foe, and, drawing that ponderous sword from its sheath, severed the giant's head from the trunk, then held it up to the view of both armies, the crash of the Israelite war-cry shook the heaven and the earth. The Philistines, confounded and utterly demoralized, waited not a moment for further fight, but fled, each man for himself, toward their cities upon the plain. The eager men of Israel poured down the valley and over the hills, pressing the pursuit beyond Gath, even to the walls of northern Ekron.

The victorious youth, returning to the camp

with the spoils of his encounter, was seized upon by Abner and brought before the king. About Saul were gathered many of the army chiefs, seasoned veterans of many campaigns; there also were the princes of the blood, and Jonathan. All gazed in admiration upon the young hero, but none appeared to know him. Who could he be that had wrought so valorous a deed for Israel this day? With a curious mixture of authority and deference, Saul demanded, "Whose son art thou, thou young man?" And the quiet, musical voice fell upon ears which had often heard it before, "I am the son of thy servant Jesse the Bethlehemite." It was David, the shepherd-musician, whose harp and voice had wrought such wonders in the palace. His long absence from the court at a period when the change in his personal appearance came most rapidly, the swiftly moving chain of exciting events, and the unaccustomed rôle which he so suddenly appeared to play, had served to prevent his recognition by Saul and his men, until, at the king's demand, he announced himself.

The eyes of Jonathan were fastened in admiration upon the manly form of the young hero. He remembered his unassuming manners at the court when he was rendering a service to the king, to the prince, and to the nation, that might have served to sound his praises over the land. He had looked upon the young harper as an upright and a pleasant lad, handsome, winning, capable, but yet only a gentle singer. Now he beheld him filled with a spirit of heroism that put to shame the greatest warriors of the nation. His mind ran back to his own youth, seemingly so far away, to that bright morning when he had said to his armor-bearer, "Let us go over to the Philistines' garrison;" "for there is no restraint to the Lord to save by many or by few." The years since then had been filled with toil and bitter disappointment. The freshness of his early faith, had it wilted under the scorching rays of trial? Had that spirit been transferred to another? Lo, he stood before him, anointed with the Spirit that crowned Israel's kings. Not a jealous thought could find harborage in the mind of the noble prince; it was open only to the emotions that love inspired. If the wearing toil of these late years had pressed down his soul, it had not blasted it. He was still the Jonathan of the early days, more steady, more reflective, but with the same open candor of mind, the same tender but manly winsomeness of heart.

Scarcely had the short conference with the king

Jonathan stepped forth to greet David

A Man of Valor

ended, when Jonathan stepped forth to greet the "son of thy servant Jesse the Bethlehemite." Not as a servant, but as an equal, he saluted him, and, with the grave yet effusive manner of the Oriental, embraced him and kissed him upon both cheeks. Then, before the eyes of the admiring soldiers, who were gathering back from the pursuit, he led him to his own tent; and when David came forth again, lo, he was clad in the royal robe of the kingdom's heir; upon his hip was girded the sword of Jonathan, and he carried in his hand that prince's bow. Thus did Jonathan seek to honor David before the people, by showing him favor such as would ordinarily be accorded to none, even of the closest kin or the greatest fame.

But to Jonathan the act meant far more. In David he had found his successor, and the Spirit within him signified that this was the "better neighbor" who should take the throne. But yet he loved him, he loved him with a deep and strong love that struck deeper and more holy chords than does even the love of woman for man. And in the secret of his pavilion he made with David a covenant of peace. Communing with him upon the future, he opened to the mind of the young shepherd things that had been vague before to him; he showed the certainty of his election to the kingdom by his anointing by Samuel, which had but a little while before taken place; and, in utter self-forgetfulness he declared to David the glory of the future. The hardship and trouble that were to come between, perhaps neither could see; but it was to the astonishment of the simple, grand-hearted young shepherd-warrior that the prince imperial should ask already of him a boon. "Jehovah be between me and thee," Jonathan said, " and between my seed and thy seed forever, and thou shalt not only while yet I live show me the kindness of Jehovah, that I die not; but also thou shalt not cut off thy kindness from my house forever; no, not when the Lord hath cut off the enemies of David every one from the face of the earth."

Twice in after years Jonathan caused David, at both times a fugitive, and seemingly helpless and at his mercy, " to swear again " the covenant which here passed between them, " because he loved him; for he loved him as he loved his own soul."

When David stepped forth with the apparel and the weapons of Jonathan upon him, it was to the army a sign of signal favor from the prince; but to Jonathan it was a token that God's

A Man of Valor

man had been found to fill the throne, and that himself, the natural heir, had abdicated in his favor, according to the will of God. Yet neither was the one puffed up, nor the other cast down, "for the soul of Jonathan was knit with the soul of David," and in likeness of spirit and equal joy of mind they clasped hands to walk together to the end.

CHAPTER VI

Intercessor and Defender

THE campaign did not end with the battle of Ephes-dammim. Saul kept the field, determined to scourge the Philistines into a peace which should be lasting. His army, in small and large detachments, was in active service for weeks, making forays into Philistine territory, smiting bands of Philistine warriors which might be caught, and terrorizing the country round about the walled cities. In these Israelite bands the youthful slayer of Goliath found opportunity to add to his laurels. His journey from Bethlehem to the camp, in charge of provisions for his brothers, proved to be his last peaceful errand. Thereafter he was a man of war. Saul, reposing in him more and more confidence, promoted him rapidly from rank to rank, until he came to hold a position in the army second only to those of the king and Jonathan.

Nor was he a favorite alone with the princes. His kindliness of heart, his sympathy with the least in rank and power, and his unfailing cheerfulness under all conditions, won to him the hearts of all the servants of Saul, common soldiers as well as officers. Even in the cities of Israel his fame spread rapidly, and the name of David was coupled with that of Saul in song and recital. That fact worked woe to the happy relations between the proud monarch and his new-made captain.

The campaign was ended; the trumpets sounded the recall to all the scattered bands; and, gathering their numbers and their pomp, the armies of Israel, with Saul, Jonathan, David, and Abner at the head, marched homeward. At every city, as they passed, an ovation awaited them. In the capital city there was preparing such a triumph as the soul of King Saul loved. The dignity, the wealth, and the beauty of the city combined to give a royal welcome to the returning heroes. As the serried columns, with martial clang of sword and shield, and deep-voiced chanting of the song of triumph, wound up the green vale from Jebus, forth from the wide-swinging gates of Gibeah issued another procession to meet them. Graybearded, reverend elders were at its head; whiteclad priests, and mothers with their children, and youths who looked for the first time upon the panoply of war, followed in the wake. Their acclaim swelled loud as they approached nearer and nearer the returning host. Then out from either side there moved, to the faster thrumming of the timbrels and the shrilling of the pipes, a company of maidens, their sweet voices rising in plainer chorus as the noise of the multitude sank, praising the deeds of the warriors and of their heads of hundreds and of thousands. At first in chorus, then in responsive parts, and again in full choir, they sang the praises of king and captain, prince and private.

The countenance of the king lighted, and glowed with high pleasure, as his eye swept over the fair array, and his ear caught the music of the song, timed to the light and graceful dance: —

> Praise ye Jehovah, the Strength of Israel,
> Whose glorious arm, whose righteous arm, o'erpowers their foes,
> > Who holds the hand of his anointed, even Saul's,
> > Who smites amain with David's falchion, and prevails!
> In the greatness of his glorious power he dashed in dust
> The iron chariots and the chains of Caphtorim!

Then sang the maidens of one company: —

> The arm of God's anointed, it is strong,
> And Saul hath slain his thousands in the field.

And the other company responded: —

A Man of Valor

> The Lord hath worked his wonders by his chosen man,
> And David hath his tens of thousands slain.
>
> Praise ye Jehovah, who hath triumphed gloriously—

swelled the full chorus of voices —

> Praise ye the Lord, who reigns in cloud and light!
> Shout the dire tidings in the streets of Gath,
> That God hath found a champion to o'ermatch her pride!

David and Saul were in every mind; they were the center of attention and the theme of song. But it was David and Saul, not Saul and David; for, "Saul hath slain his thousands, and David his ten thousands," chanted the maidens.

The ear of Jonathan, quick to catch the praises of his friend, was charged also to note any ill-advised word that might carry to his father's mind a suspicion of the secret which he himself bore, the secret that the dreaded "neighbor" who should take the throne, was found. As the maidens sang, "Saul hath slain his thousands, and David his ten thousands," he shot a quick glance at his father, and was dismayed to see a flush of anger overspread the king's face. Saul had noted, and with ready suspicion interpreted. "Hearest thou that, Jonathan?" he demanded. "They have ascribed unto David ten thousands, and to me they have ascribed but thousands! and what can he have more but the kingdom?" His gaze shifted to the face of David, who, modestly bearing his honors, seemed little to notice the lavish praise; and a look of mingled gloom and hatred settled upon the king's countenance. He received with ungracious looks the homage that his people offered him, and entered the gates of the city with a sullen mien.

In Jonathan's mind that look and that exclamation were the heralds of evil quickly to come. The night was one of little rest for him. He held no jealous thoughts. The people's praises, indeed, had not been shouted for him; no loudly intoned triumph song had extolled his prowess on the battle-field; no voice had been raised to tell of his sleepless watchings, his prayers, his labors. The hero of Michmash had been eclipsed by the victor of Ephes-dammim; and, more, he knew that that new favorite should yet take his place upon the throne. But he did not mourn for his departed popularity, nor were his thoughts at all of himself. His wakefulness had other cause. In another room his father, in his uneasy sleep, was muttering curses on the son of Jesse, and

A Man of Valor

tossing in the rising fever of a tortured mind. Again must Jonathan stand by the side of a madman, to calm if possible, to shield in any event. And would the gentle harper of those earlier days have still his mysterious power upon that disturbed mind? Who could forecast the evil that lay beyond the curtain of this night?

In the morning the king was raging. Jonathan was called early to his father's side, and, sending for David, begged him to take his harp, as of old, and try to charm away the evil spirit. A harp was brought, and the fingers that had so lately clutched the sword came back with their wonted skill to the trembling strings of the instrument. The strong, sweet voice struck in:—

> My voice shalt thou hear in the morning, O Lord,
>> In the morning will I direct my prayer unto thee, and will look up.
>
> For thou art not a God that hath pleasure in wickedness;
>> Neither shall evil dwell with thee.
>
> The arrogant shall not stand in thy sight:
>> Thou hatest all workers of iniquity.
>
> Thou wilt destroy them that speak lies:
>> The Lord abhorreth the bloody and deceitful man.
>
> But as for me, in the multitude of thy lovingkindness will I come into thy house:
>> In thy fear will I worship toward thy holy temple.

The king was listening with an intentness that presaged good; and Jonathan, slipping out, left the musician almost alone with the king, to complete the cure. The voice sank to a gentle invocation,—

> Lead me, O Lord, in thy righteousness because of mine enemies;
> Make thy way plain before my face.

Into the eyes of the king came a baleful light; for this to him seemed a prayer for David against himself; and as, with the ring of righteous indignation, the song rose higher,—

> Destroy thou them, O God;
> Let them fall by their own counsel;
> Thrust them out in the multitude of their transgressions;
> For they have rebelled against thee —

Saul, giving his ungrounded suspicions full sway, lashed his mind into a frenzy, and gripped the javelin by his side with a furious and scarcely suppressed rage. But the glad voice, soaring on to a triumphant close, declared,—

> For thou, Lord, wilt bless the righteous;
> With favor wilt thou compass him as with a shield.

To the maddened king this seemed direct defi-

A Man of Valor

ance. Starting to his feet, he hurled his javelin straight at the heart of David. The quick-eyed youth let fall his harp and stepped to one side, yet almost received the deadly thrust of the javelin as it sped by him and struck in the wall behind. Quickly he escaped from the king's presence.

The cure had failed at last. In rage at his physician, the king had steeled his mind against the soothing influence of his music, and thereafter he was more and more given up to the malign impulsion of the evil spirit, and sank more rapidly and hopelessly into the depths of his madness.

Yet that murderous attack upon his harper, so unexpected, was deemed but the act of one made irresponsible by a temporary fit of madness. With the cunning of a disordered mind, Saul took advantage of that impression, and veiled his enmity, that he might make more sure of his victim. Thereafter he professed the greatest friendship for David, and the young man was an honored guest at the palace, and increasingly a favorite with all the people.

Chiefest of all his pleasure, however, was his association with the prince. Not merely companions in moments of pleasure and recreation were they. If side by side they stood as their bow-strings twanged in the archery contests, they also planned in the camp the disposition of troops and the fortification of mountain passes. If arm in arm they paced the terraces in the royal gardens, or pledged each other at the public feasts, they spent also many an hour in counsel and in prayer over the affairs of the nation. Here the king-to-be received from his royal friend and tutor many a lesson in statecraft and diplomacy. In the train of Jonathan he came into contact with embassies of other nations, and not infrequently was detailed to employ his talents in important public affairs. And the communion of these two, thus so strangely mated, grew deeper and stronger with the days.

But the watchful eye of Saul would not long permit this intimacy. His jealousy of the young Bethlehemite, feeding in silence, became ever stronger and less controllable. He grew more and more certain, though he knew nothing of what Jonathan knew, that this young golden-haired hero, shining like an angel in the setting of his court, was destined for the throne. And with the growing certainty came an insane and unreasoning determination to prevent it. He did not pause to think that whom God had chosen, him He would protect. He had not been trained to see omnipotence in God and helplessness in man. So he plotted, and expected by his plots to thwart the purpose of God.

Yet he despised himself for his attempt upon the life of David. He thought it truly to be an unkinglike act for a sovereign to assassinate a subject. Besides, he dared not yet stand in the eyes of the people as the slayer of the popular and blameless young warrior. So he said to himself, " Let not mine hand be upon him, but let the hand of the Philistines be upon him." He loaded David with compliments, praised him for his conduct in the face of the enemy, and encouraged him to make more determined war upon the Philistines.

Again the bands of Israel went forth, under David, and fought with the Philistines. The result of the war was only to raise David higher in the esteem of men as a skilful captain and warrior, daring in plan and dauntless in execution. And as at the beginning, so now, the women sang his praises.

Among the maidens of the court the proud and beautiful Michal held chief rank. She was the king's daughter, and her own powers of mind and her charm of manner made her a place no other could fill. Yet she was very different from her brother Jonathan. She had most of Saul's qualities, and few of Ahinoam's. Beautiful, graceful, accomplished, she was sometimes gracious and sometimes haughty; swayed sometimes by love and sometimes by passion; fearing to run no danger when her heart or her mind demanded it, but controlled most often by a love of praise; and in matters of religion guided more by a sense of propriety than by a feeling of devotion.

She loved David. His valor, his grace, his accomplishments, fascinated her, and through Jonathan she was continually hearing his praises sung.

The report of this attachment, circulating through palace, city, and camp, was brought to the ears of Saul by his courtiers. Saul welcomed the report; for, knowing his daughter, he believed he might reckon upon her loyalty to himself against her faithfulness to her husband. And he arranged for the marriage. But he reckoned ill; for Michal really loved David; and henceforth Saul found two of his own household arrayed against him on the side of David: one open-faced, unsuspecting, fearless; the other subtle, discerning, and crafty. Whatever he planned, the mad king found himself thwarted.

A Man of Valor

At last his jealousy could no longer contain itself within the bounds of assumed benevolence. The border war with the Philistines still continued; and one morning, while the council was being held in the palace, news was brought of the return the previous night of the Hebrew band under David, fresh from recent victories. The admiration of some of the councilors would not be restrained, and, with no thought of incurring displeasure from his king and father-in-law, they openly lauded David for his skill and valor.

The king was maddened. He broke forth into a fierce tirade against his captain-in-chief, that dog of a Bethlehemite, who was grasping eagerly at all the laurels he could reach, and who doubtless was aiming at the throne. He openly declared his wish that the son of Jesse should die, and to Jonathan himself and to all his servants he gave a charge that, seeing David, they should slay him. The power of the evil spirit was upon his mind, and its fury shone through his eyes, so that not one of his men dared answer him. Nor did Jonathan attempt to speak for his friend, but, hastening away, he sought David, to acquaint him with this open danger.

He found him in his house, overlooking the plain below, where were encamped the guards of the king, and his own band. "Take heed to thyself," said Jonathan to David, "until the morning, and abide in a secret place, and hide thyself; and I will go out and stand beside my father in the field where thou art, and I will commune with my father of thee; and what I see, that I will tell thee."

The following day the king was to review his troops upon the parade-ground, and the prince was in attendance upon him, with all the officers of the court. But the king did not go down. Instead, he sent his officers forward to the grounds, and, going out upon the upper terrace of his palace porch, he stood alone with Jonathan, watching the evolutions of the companies below. His mood had changed; the sight of his warriors awakened memories of glorious deeds, and he conversed with Jonathan upon the exploits of different ones whom they could recognize at the head of the troops,— Ahiezer and Joash, brothers of Benjamin, Adnah the Manassite, and Amasai of Judah. Abner, too, the chief, of him they spoke, and of the energetic pursuit he led after Ephes-dammim.

Thus naturally their thoughts drifted upon David and his deeds. And Jonathan, standing there alone with his father in quietness, "spake

He stood alone with Jonathan

A Man of Valor

good of David," and said, "Let not the king sin against his servant, against David; because he hath not sinned against thee, and because his works have been to thee-ward very good; for he did put his life in his hand, and slew the Philistine, and Jehovah wrought a great salvation for all Israel; thou sawest it, and didst rejoice; wherefore then wilt thou sin against innocent blood, to slay David without a cause?"

The king's heart was touched. Standing alone upon that height, they seemed lifted above the petty troubles that hung like clouds upon the plain. The voice of Jonathan, tender and persuasive in his self-forgetting eloquence, carried the king beyond and above his natural self, and he answered impulsively, "As Jehovah liveth, he shall not be slain." So saying, he turned abruptly, and passed within the door.

With the good news, Jonathan hastened to David's place of concealment in the plain, near which he had expected to interview his father. There he sought to reassure David with his own confidence of safety, and urged him to take this propitious moment for presentation to the king. So they went together to the audience chamber, and there, in the presence of those who had the day before received a charge to kill him, David came before Saul, who received him graciously, and listened to his report of recent operations in the field.

Shortly after, David was again called into action, and again was victor in a great battle with the Philistines. Returning to Gibeah, he took his accustomed place in the court, unconscious of the effect his exploit had had upon Saul. But he was quickly made to feel how uncertain a position he held in the mind of his king. As on a previous occasion, he was playing upon his harp one evening before the king, when Saul again in a sudden fury cast his javelin at him. An angel of God turned the weapon aside, and David, slipping away, made haste through the dark streets to his home. There Michal, coming from the palace, shortly joined him, and declared to him, " If thou save not thy life to-night, to-morrow thou wilt be slain." Even as they conversed, they heard the voices of the watchmen set about the house as guards until the morning. The city gates were shut and guarded; but their house was built against the city wall, looking out upon the valley; and down that steep height, in the dead of night, the faithful Michal, like that ancestress of David's in Jericho long before, with cords let down the fugitive outside the walls.

A Man of Valor

Where should he go? He felt that Jonathan could not protect him; he was afraid to draw the wrath of Saul on his family at Bethlehem. But Samuel — there was a safe refuge with one who feared no king, and who had himself anointed David for the royal seat. He needed a hasty refuge; for should he, alone, attempt now this place of concealment, now that, how easily might Saul pursue and take him in his confusion! So he turned his hurried steps toward Ramah, about three miles to the north, and there before the morning he found safety under the protection of the great prophet.[4]

In the morning the guards, invading the house, even to the bedchamber, found that David had fled. Their report to the king resulted in the summoning of Michal. She came undaunted; but before the furious appearance of her father she quailed, and, scrupulous of nothing, to save herself declared that she had sought to detain her husband, but had been forced by threat of death to aid him.

Saul was determined to take David even from under the protecting hand of Samuel, and no sooner had word been brought that David was with Samuel in the community of the prophets

---
[4] See Note 4, Appendix.

at Ramah, than he sent messengers charged to take him.

The schools which Samuel had established in Israel were composed of young men, known as sons of the prophets, who under their instructors studied the law, sacred history, music, and poetry. They supported themselves largely by tilling the soil, and they built their own dwellings. These dwellings (called Naioth, "booths") were for the most part very simple, and were set down outside the cities, in the midst of nature, where, in the quiet and beauty of natural surroundings, the Spirit of God could speak to the soul. Their music and their composition of sacred poetry were a part at once of the students' worship and their study. Under the influence of their holy song, the Spirit of God often rested upon them, and they continued, in high poetical strain, to prophesy of the future of Israel, of the coming of the Messiah, and of the final redemption of all from sin. In this school David had received much of the inspiration and power which were so manifest in the control of Saul's evil spirit. So it continued through all the history of these schools of the prophets: in Elisha's time we hear him calling for a minstrel to play upon the harp in order that the spirit of prophecy might come upon him.

It was into the presence of such a company and of such a service, controlled and inspired by the Spirit of God, that the messengers of Saul came to arrest David. But no sooner were they in the presence of Samuel and his students than the Spirit overcame them, and they joined with them in song and prophecy. The word was carried to Saul. Blinded by his rage, he sent a second company, and even a third, upon the same errand. Then, finding the messengers a vain reliance, he rose, and, with murder in his heart, came himself to Ramah, determined to stride into the midst of the assembly, and, in the presence of Samuel and all the prophets, with his own hand to kill David.

But on the way the mysterious influence fell also upon him, and when he came into the presence of Samuel, it was not with curses, but with blessings; not with threats of vengeance, but with prophecies of a forgiving Saviour. And there, casting aside his royal robes, and by the power of God upon him falling down in their midst, he lay in the private dress of a common man all the rest of that day and that night, like one in a sacred trance.

The word spread far and wide, and the people were drawn together in Naioth to see their king so strangely comporting himself with the prophets. The word was carried to Gibeah. Among the pious there was a doubtful joy, among the lighter of mind consternation, but nowhere was there derision. Again, as in the happier time of the early kinghood, it was said among the people, "Is Saul also among the prophets?"

How strangely sad must have been that familiar question to Jonathan, "Is Saul also among the prophets?" calling up memories of the happy days when his father and mother gathered himself and his brothers and sisters around them, in the humbler home of Gibeah, and told them of the wondrous honor that had come by the word of the Lord through his prophet. How strange a gleam of brightness that well-remembered proverb now cast upon the somber scene, where demons were struggling for the possession of a soul and a kingdom! The once glad-hearted, happy prince was bowing beneath a load of care and anxiety. His heavy, lustrous locks were worn away from his forehead, and the pencil of time had been at work upon his eyes and brow.

Several times in the last few years there had come tokens of promise, which the eager hopes of the prince had seized, that the malady of the king was stopped. With time had come even a

A Man of Valor

heavier disappointment. Did the present experience warrant the building again of hopes for Saul? He was in the presence of Samuel; his mind had been seized and used by the Spirit of God, as it had been in the early days. Would not the reformation be complete and permanent? Rumor came quickly the next day that the king had awakened from his trance subdued and humble; that, in the presence of Samuel, he had made reconciliation with David; and that he stayed to listen to the counsels of the prophet. Jonathan believed, hoped, trusted.

But upon the heels of the report came David in person. Bursting into the presence of the prince, he demanded, "What have I done? what is mine iniquity? and what is my sin before thy father, that he seeketh my life?" Jonathan was astonished at the vehemence of his friend, so out of keeping, it seemed, with the present circumstances. "God forbid," he answered, solemnly and soothingly; "thou shalt not die: behold, my father will do nothing either great or small, but that he will show it me; and why should my father hide this thing from me? it is not so."

But David would not be reassured. Who, indeed, could trust such a man as Saul? Impressed one day with the Spirit of God to reconciliation, he would break out the next in the most furious attempts at murder. And David had seen that morning in the leaden eye of the king at Ramah, a smoldering fire of vengeance not yet extinguished. "Truly as the Lord liveth, and as thy soul liveth," he declared to Jonathan, "there is but a step between me and death." "Whatsoever thy soul desireth, I will even do it for thee," responded Jonathan.

Then David unfolded a plan to test the king's sincerity. The next day began the three days' feast of the new moon, at which all the immediate members of the king's family and court were expected to be present. David proposed that Jonathan grant him leave to go home to Bethlehem, and see what effect his absence would have upon the mind of the king. So wrought upon were the young man's feelings that at the close of his speech, he was almost ready to accuse Jonathan himself of treachery. "Deal kindly with thy servant," he implored: "for thou hast brought thy servant into a covenant of the Lord with thee; notwithstanding, if there be in me iniquity, slay me thyself; for why shouldest thou bring me to thy father?" "Far be that thought from thee!" exclaimed Jonathan. "If I should know at all that evil were determined by my father to come

A Man of Valor 131

upon thee, then would not I tell it thee?" David objected still more excitedly, "Who shall tell me? or what if thy father answer thee roughly?"

The tension was becoming too great. The great-hearted prince, himself imperturbable under all dangers, could yet sympathize with his suffering friend. Throwing his arm over the other's shoulder, he said, "Come, and let us go out into the field." So they passed together for the last time through the streets of Gibeah, the hand of one upon the arm of the other, and both, absorbed in thought, quite oblivious of the attention they attracted from street and gate, housetop and window.

The companionship of the prince on the long walk to the valley had calmed the mind of David, and there again they two swore the oath of eternal friendship that first they took in the tent at Ephes-dammim. Standing beside his younger friend, with his hand laid upon his, Jonathan lifted up his eyes to heaven, and addressed David in words that were at first a prayer to God: "O Lord God of Israel, when I have sounded my father about to-morrow any time, or the third day, and, behold, if there be good toward David, and I then send not unto thee, and show it thee; the Lord do so and much more to Jonathan; but if it please my father to do thee evil, then I will show it thee, and send thee away, that thou mayest go in peace; and the Lord be with thee, as he hath been with my father." The voice of the prince, in that last pitiful allusion to happier days, sank low, as if whispering a prayer for the present good of the king. To David he continued, "And thou shalt not only while yet I live show me the kindness of the Lord, that I die not; but also thou shalt not cut off thy kindness from my house forever; no, not when the Lord hath cut off the enemies of David every one from the face of the earth."

So with the shadow of a great sorrow hanging over them, those two young men stood under the open sky, binding themselves before God in a covenant for a future whose secrets they could not guess, a covenant the fruits of which were to be gathered long after only by the pitifully maimed son of the elder.

Then Jonathan said to David, "To-morrow is the [feast of the] new moon; and thou wilt be missed, because thy seat will be empty. And when thou hast stayed three days, thou shalt go down quickly, and come to the place where thou didst hide thyself when the business [of the previous reconciliation] was in hand, and shalt remain by the stone that showeth the way. And I will shoot three arrows on the side thereof, as though I shot at a mark. And, behold, I will send a lad, saying, Go, find the arrows. If I say unto the lad, Behold, the arrows are on this side of thee, take them; then come thou; for there is peace to thee, and no hurt; as the Lord liveth. But if I say thus unto the young man, Behold, the arrows are beyond thee; go thy way; for the Lord hath sent thee away. And as touching the matter which thou and I have spoken of, behold, the Lord be between thee and me forever." Thus touchingly alluding to that sacred bond between them, Jonathan parted from David.

The same day came Saul; and on the morrow the feast was spread in the palace. At the royal table there were places for four. Saul sat at the head, and Abner sat at his side. Opposite sat Jonathan; but David's place by his side was empty. The feast went on with no mention of the absent member; the hum of conversation rose and sank, now upon the camp and battle, now upon the purposes of the feast, now an interchange of inquiries and felicities, but never a mention of David. Jonathan was encouraged; but could he have read the heart of his father, far different would have been his feelings; for the king was saying over and over to himself, " Something hath befallen him, he is not clean; surely he is not clean "— meaning that, according to the provisions of the ceremonial law, some defilement, as the touching of a dead body, had debarred him from the feast until the evening.

But the second day he marked again the absence of David, and, fearing at last that it was by design, he could no longer contain his suspicions, yet endeavored to conceal them under an indifferent manner. "Wherefore," he inquired carelessly of Jonathan, "cometh not the son of Jesse to meat, neither yesterday, nor to-day?" Then, despite himself, his eyes fastened with intensity upon Jonathan, while that young man endeavored to answer with the same ease: "David earnestly asked leave of me to go to Bethlehem; and he said, Let me go, I pray thee; for our family hath a sacrifice in the city; and my brother, he hath commanded me to be there; and now, if I have found favor in thine eyes, let me get away, I pray thee, and see my brethren. Therefore," concluded Jonathan, "he cometh not unto the king's table."

For the first time in his life, the king's ungovernable rage was turned upon Jonathan. White-faced and trembling with passion, he denounced this most loved and honored of his sons in the vilest terms. He cursed him as a fool who could

not see the evident designs of one who would steal
away his throne. He cursed his own wife, his
son's mother,— the deepest and foulest insult an
Oriental can heap upon another. And he concluded with this demand, "Wherefore now send
and fetch him unto me, for he shall surely die."

The crisis had come: there was no way but to
meet it. To all that torrent of scandalous abuse
and personal insult, the spirit of the hero prince
rose superior. He answered not a word in defense
of himself. But for David,— steadily meeting
the eye of his father, he asked, in level, dispas-
sionate tones, "Wherefore shall he be slain? what
hath he done?"

The frame of Saul vibrated with wrath. From
out his livid face burned like two great coals his
flaming eyes. It was a demon that started from
the chair of state, and, unable to articulate a syl-
lable, drew back the spear-arm, and cast his javelin straight at his son.

Then the blood of the Benjamite leaped to the
cheek of Jonathan, and in fierce anger he rose
from the table. The hand of an angel had turned
aside the weapon, and prevented a deed that would
have killed the doer also. Not for himself did
Jonathan burn with anger, but because he saw
thereby that "it was determined of his father to

slay David." Self-forgetfulness never was shown more; righteous anger never had a more unselfish cause.

The next morning the prince passed out of the gate, only a little lad being with him to carry his bow and arrows. He was going out, as was his custom, said the people, to practise archery in the field. But he did not stay upon the practise grounds immediately below the city. Striking down the valley, he passed along, apparently sunk in deep, grief-filled thought. The lad followed him wonderingly. They were coming near to the road that branched off between the hills, past Nob, to Ajalon and the Philistine cities. There a great stone stood at the turning of the way, and upon it were marked, facing the road, two names, with hands pointing in opposite directions: "Hebron," "Shechem," the two cities of refuge, toward the south and the north respectively.[5]

Just before reaching the stone, Jonathan stopped, and took his bow and arrows from the hand of the lad, telling him to run forward to gather the arrows he should shoot. As the lad darted forward, Jonathan shot an arrow over him, and called aloud, "Is not the arrow beyond thee?" And then, "Make speed, haste, stay not."

---
[5] See Note 5, Appendix.

The words were for David, but the lad knew nothing of that. As he found the arrows which Jonathan shot quickly one after another, and brought them back, he was still further mystified to be given his master's weapons and told to take them home. Short sport, indeed, he thought. But he went obediently.

Then David rose up from his hiding-place and came forward. His short visit home, although he was in suspense, had given his mind time for settlement, and now, his unworthy suspicions of Jonathan being proved groundless by such whole-hearted devotion, David acknowledged at once his gratitude and his loyalty to his prince, by bowing before him to the ground. Jonathan tenderly lifted him up and kissed him. Few were their words; for words could not tell the depth of their sorrow. They "wept one with another, until David exceeded." Then Jonathan said to David, "Go in peace, forasmuch as we have sworn both of us in the name of the Lord, saying, The Lord be between me and thee, and between my seed and thy seed forever."

With a last lingering hand-clasp, they took leave, and turned each to his way — the one to the city that represented the glory and splendor of Israel, and that stood on the way to humiliation and death; the other toward the wilderness, or a foreign land, a way that led to the throne. Once they turned to signal a last farewell, and the prince saw the young Bethlehemite, his brother, pass out of sight toward Nob.

CHAPTER VII

In Palace and Wood

THE royal palace in Gibeah made no such architectural pretensions as later reigns were to see; yet in size and embellishment it far exceeded any house of a ruler or great man before known to Israel. Its site was the most commanding: upon the gently rounded hill that topped the steep cliff, it stood and looked over valley and hill, to the seas of the East and the West, and the cities of the kingdom that crowded the landscape on either side.

The sloping ground had offered to the Hebrew architects a tempting opportunity to use their favorite terrace plan, and the marble and cedar porches that rose one above and behind another, showed like a snowy wood in front of the king's house.

Upon the side of the town the palace walls maintained completely the look of Oriental seclusiveness. Neither gardens nor walks relieved the somber face of its piled-up masonry. Here and there in the face of its lofty upper story were latticed windows, for the most part projected from

the wall. Below, there was only the opening of
the gate, here in the palace widened beyond that
of the ordinary dwelling, and guarded by heavy
iron doors, with bars upon the inner side that
shot clear across from post to post. The impression of privacy was maintained, notwithstanding
this wide aperture, by a cross wall a little way
within, that shut from view all the interior might
contain. The passage, dividing, turned to the left
and the right, and then straight forward again
these two led into the interior.

This outer passage, which in space was not inconsiderable, was, in the days when the king sat
for judgment, not infrequently crowded by persons seeking justice. High and low pressed along
the narrow street up to the palace gate, through
which they were admitted by the royal guards as
the press within would permit.

Directly in front of the gate, and against the
cross-wall before mentioned, was usually seated
some one of the king's official family whom he
had delegated to receive and sift all cases. Such
as this official could himself settle were dismissed;
those pleaders who must see the king were allowed
to go within. Through one of the passages they
were conducted for a short distance, until it ended
in a large interior court, where something of the

A Man of Valor 141

magnificence of the royal abode began to be seen.

The court was for the most part paved with mosaic of different colored stones. In its center rose a fountain in several jets and sprays; and on either side of this, in specially enriched plats of ground, two graceful palms uplifted their heads, in the midst of flowers, low shrubs, and trailing vines.

On the side of the court opposite the entrances was the audience-chamber of the king. It was open in front, the building above being supported by polished cedar pillars; and it was lighted from without wholly by its open side toward the court. Here, on audience days, in a chair of state, or throne, sat the king, to receive embassies and private petitioners. On the other sides of the court were rooms used for private conferences, for the retirement of the elders and councilors, and for other state purposes.

Above this first floor, and reached by two flights of stone steps, was an open gallery, which extended completely around the court. Behind this were private rooms for the accommodation of many members of the court, and for visitors of distinction. The flat tile-and-earth-covered roof was reached by a continuation of one of these staircases. Upon this roof, in different places, were built isolated chambers. The spaces between were often, in the hot season, covered over with awnings, as well as by vines trained upon supports, giving coolness and seclusion to those who wished to rest.

Returning now to the ground floor, we have time for a more leisurely survey of this interior of the building. The scarcely awakened art of the Hebrew architect had been spent upon its decoration. From floor to parapet there was a lavish display of splendor, in the chalky white and dull red of the Jebus sandstones and the black of basalt upon the court flagging; in the lustrous dark red of cedar and the gleaming whiteness of marble on the pillars, balustrades, and stairs; and in the gold that adorned the carvings and the elaborate fresco work of the walls and arches.

The entrances to the rooms upon the sides were closed to prying eyes, not by doors, but by heavy, rich-colored curtains, harmonizing, in their crimson and scarlet and in their heavy texture, with the richness and massiveness of the general scheme.

The audience-chamber had received the greatest care in its construction and decoration. Its floor was a platform raised slightly above the court, and upon a dais at the farther end stood the chair of state — a throne unpretentious enough when compared with that of Solomon two generations later, or even with those of neighboring kings of that time, yet carrying enough of the sense of majesty and glory to the eyes of a nation of shepherds and husbandmen. Flanking it on either side were two alabaster pedestals, surmounted by golden candlesticks, that furnished, on dark days, the needed light, which, reflected from the gold and polished stone of ceiling and walls, gave treble value to the scant magnificence. A low, cushioned divan ran on two sides of the room, intended, however, not for visitors and petitioners, except by special grace of the king, but for the councilors and officers of the royal household.

Without, the brown and green of the towering palms, with the flowers and low trailing vines at their feet, in the midst of which jetted and splashed the fountain, gave that touch which nature must supply to relieve the labored efforts of man for the beautifying of his surroundings.

At either of the far corners of the court we observe the openings of two passages, curtained like the other doors. These lead to the more private parts of the palace, courts much like that we have seen, only more homelike and retired in their greater display of greenery and greater number of appliances for private comfort. Here, each in their own apartments, dwelt the families of the king and his sons.

Grouped around each of these courts there were, below, besides a guest-chamber similar to the audience-room in the outer court, the open-sided kitchens of the household, and various rooms for storage of food supplies and of fuel. Above were the private rooms of the members of the family. The most of the farther rooms looked out through the porches, or above them, over the wide prospect of the country of Benjamin and the neighboring tribes. Passages led also from these inner courts to the terraces and gardens, and from one court to another. The jealousy of the modern Eastern harem, in which the privacy of the family is guarded as the mysteries in a sacred temple, was modified in the ancient Israelitish family, where women enjoyed a liberty unknown in most Oriental countries, and joined with their fathers, brothers, and husbands in the reception at least of family friends.

It was, indeed, in the cool of these inner courts, amid the shade-trees and vines and the plashing fountains, that gatherings for private and social intercourse were held. And not only friends, but messengers and couriers, might be admitted here

A Man of Valor

to make their reports, should the master of the house be found therein.

Here, on an ominous morning, was Jonathan seated in deep meditation. The crescent register of the sun-dial, perched high on the northern wall of the court, smiling down its fleeting tidings to the garden, spoke now of nearing noon, when men and women of that clime bethink themselves of resting in the cool of their breezy chambers. All the morning had the usually active prince remained here in his garden court, now reclining upon the raised and cushioned pavement beside the fountain, now restlessly pacing to and fro, now attending, with fond but preoccupied look, to the play and the prattle of his little son, who kept him guileless company. The boy, indeed, had guided much of the thought of that undisturbed morning.

Many years had passed since that day when Michmash and Beth-Horon had clasped their arms about the undying deeds of the king's son. Then we knew him as a beardless youth; now he appears a man of grave and worn aspect, with full dark beard hiding the strengthened lines of the lower face, and eyes that, like the guarded gate of the palace, speak only to the intimate of the glory within. Over his shoulders still fall, indeed, the lustrous wavy billows of his hair, yet showing prematurely, in his fewer than forty years, the ravages that care, the ally of time, offers as a trophy to the devourer of men.

Sad were the thoughts that had mostly occupied the mind of the royal thinker this day. Upon the shaded pavement little Mephibosheth played, crowing and catching at the sunny patches which the broad fig leaves permitted now and again to fall upon his three-cubit domain — sun-favors that danced and dallied or sped away and disappeared, but always, whether speeding or staying, sure to elude the grasp of the tiny hand that thought them waiting to be picked up. So, even, so, had the sun-kisses of mortal happiness played with the greater hand: fair, inviting, and free they seemed for the quick clutch, but they always slipped away or tantalizingly remained to dance upon the empty fist. The glory of the kingdom of war: at Jabesh-Gilead it had seemed glory; now the king of the realm was exercising his veterans in the pursuit of a pitiful band of persecuted outlaws. The glory of the kingdom of state: to bring the envoys of Egypt and Phenicia to crowd the gates of Israel's capital had once seemed worthy; now their presence and their influence were an insult and a curse. The glory of the

Upon the shaded pavement little Mephibosheth played

kingdom of justice: to relieve the needy, to right oppression, to sow peace and love throughout the realm, that surely had been glorious; but now the sickening scenes that the monarch's "justice" had produced cried aloud in blood-drenched tones to the gates of God's heaven.

Yonder across the vales and hills Gibeon lay in her ruins, smitten by the hand of Saul, who in his effort to placate Heaven by destroying the evil from out the land, had trampled upon the ancient pact of Gilgal. More horrible still, on the left yet smoked the city of the priests, whose devoted inhabitants — men, women, and little children — Saul had slain by the hand of his evil herd-master Doeg. Yes, even that venerable man, the high priest Ahimelech, who in his childhood had been at once the rival and the friend of the young Benjamite Saul,— against him the crazed king had not scrupled to lift his crime-stained hand, and hurry with him to death all his family and his city; for the mischievous tongue of the Edomite Doeg had denounced the high priest as a partizan and abettor of the fugitive David.

And David was in hiding. Where? The prince's step, that had sounded so rapidly upon the flagging as he recounted the evils and the wrongs of the realm, slowed as his mind came back to his friend. He had heard of him first, after they parted, as being in the country of his enemies the Philistines; then, through one of the sons of the prophets, he learned that he had returned and taken into Moab his aged father and mother; and then that he was once more to be found in the forest and cave strongholds of the hill country of Judah, where hundreds of men, fleeing from the oppression and lack of justice in Israel, resorted to him. Later had he heard,— had all the court and country heard, indeed,— that with his band David had rescued Keilah, a Judean city beleaguered by the Philistines, and that for a time he stayed therein. At the word, Saul had called about him a considerable army, purposing to take him while shut in by the walls and gates of Keilah. But before his preparations were complete, again the word came that David had escaped, and was hiding in his well-explored fastnesses of rock and forest.

Strange indeed it appeared to Saul that all the movements of David should seem to be made in foreknowledge of the king's intentions. Such knowledge, he reasoned within himself, could come only through systematic, persistent betrayal of his secrets to him he counted his enemy. Upon all about him fell his suspicion, and he pointed it at last toward Jonathan, suggesting, by his inquiries among his followers, that they accuse his son to him. It had been upon an occasion when Saul gave utterance to such a thought, that the crafty Doeg had fastened on the priests the accusation which resulted in the terrible destruction of Nob. But none would or could accuse Jonathan.

Yet if Jonathan was guiltless of warning his wronged and hunted friend, it was not from desire. Gladly would he have cheered and saved David had it been possible, or have sent him messages of help could he have been sure of a messenger. But the threats and the cajolements of Saul had filled so many minds that those who remembered with friendly thoughts the young Bethlehemite captain were afraid to venture life in their declaration, and not often was it that Jonathan could hear more than the most uncertain rumors of the movements of his friend. Yet what he could do he did. A few there were about him who were loyal to him, to their old-time captain, and to the friendship they knew existed between those two. Such were Ahiezer and Joash, sons of Shemaah in Gibeah, and others of less note, who occasionally could act as scouts and messengers for the prince.

For such a message from one of these was he

now waiting. He had sent two of them several days before on an ostensible mission to Hebron, but with secret instructions to find out the present whereabouts of David, and to bring him word. Before they returned, one of the many emissaries whom Saul had abroad, charged with the same purpose, informed the king; and it was now the second day after Saul, trusting the information brought him, had set forth with a chosen band to seek David in the forests of Ziph, to the south of Hebron. His mind was now wholly given up to the pursuit of this one object, to find his hated rival and execute vengeance upon him. The care of the kingdom he left to his eldest son and his councilors: his mission was to slay David.

Little Mephibosheth had fallen asleep. A wandering cloud had blotted out his playthings,— the sunbeams and shadows,— and, wearied with waiting for his nurse, who did not come, he sleepily tipped over upon his cushions by the fountain-side, and knew no more of fair promises and black deceptions: unless, it might be, his dreams yet made fact of fancy; for around his lips there played fleeting little smiles, alternating with tiny frowns between his eyes, and one baby hand lay yet open and seeming to reach toward the playthings of an hour ago. The sun-dial, touched for

A Man of Valor

a moment by its master through a rift of the cloud, proclaimed the hour of rest gone by.

The sound of a firm-treading foot in the corridor announced the coming of a visitor; and, ushered in by a soft-stepping domestic, a young man in soldier's garb appeared and bowed before the prince, whose eyes shone a welcome as he recognized one of the brothers whom he had sent to Hebron.

"Pelet, thou hast tarried," said the prince. "Yet, thy mission was difficult. What news hast thou of David? and where is thy brother, Jeziel?"

"The son of Jesse, indeed, have we not seen," answered the scout; "for he keepeth himself close, and few be they that see his face. Yet while I tarried on my mission in Hebron, my brother was made a guest at Carmel by Nabal, the prince of sheepmasters, and by his wife Abigail, a woman in whom prudence dwells. And of the young men the keepers, my brother was told that David lieth in the wood that is beyond Ziph, and also to the south. And of this the young men are well aware, for the men of David company often with them, and are a guard to them against the sons of Ishmael. My brother tarries now at Hebron, while I come to thee."

"Thou hast done well, Pelet," answered the

prince. "Return now to thy father's house. Thou shalt not be forgotten when again I have need of a valiant man."

Two more points upon the dial had not been cast when the highway that led to Hebron saw a muffled figure upon a fleet dromedary speeding toward the south. Nob in its ruins, Jebus in its heathen pride, Bethlehem in its security, saw the swift passing of the seeming courier; but the mystery of his message or his person was not unveiled. The hand that held the rein and the head that turned neither to right nor left, returned not the wayfarer's salute; the eyes that burned above the muffling folds of the mantle were set steadily toward the south. The sun sank slowly down toward the western hills, yet almost seemed to stay its progress as the soft padded footfalls of the camel sounded nearer, nearer, nearer Hebron. But when the hard-pressed and jaded beast brought his rider through the vineyards and groves near to the gate of that great city, the last rays of the sun were fading off the hilltops on the north, and the busy life of the city's suburbs was withdrawing within the sheltering walls.

The shadows of city and hills were blending and deepening when the southern gate, opening to unusual authority, let forth two stalwart forms,

A Man of Valor

that without pausing took the winding road to the southeast, and were quickly swallowed up in the darkness.

.   .   .   .   .

Far within the depths of the green oak forest, in a little rock-strewn, wooded valley, a band of armed men were reposing in rough comfort upon the ground. Their score of camp-fires were sinking down into glowing beds, and the murmur of voices was gradually dying out. Clasped in the embrace of the high hills on either side, the little band, used to adventure and peril, felt themselves safer than within the walls of a city. With the bright shining of the stars above, and the deep silence of the night brooding over the forest and the rocks about them, deeper grew the influence of their evening hymn, which had so lately wakened the echoes of the surrounding cliffs: —

> I will lift up mine eyes unto the hills:
> From whence shall my help come?
> My help cometh from the Lord,
> Which made heaven and earth.
>
> He will not suffer thy foot to be moved;
> He that keepeth thee will not slumber;
> Behold, he that keepeth Israel
> Shall neither slumber nor sleep.

> The Lord is thy keeper,
> The Lord is thy shade upon thy right hand:
> The sun shall not smite thee by day,
> Nor the moon by night.
>
> The Lord shall keep thee from all evil;
> He shall keep thy soul.
> The Lord shall keep thy going out and thy coming in
> From this time forth and forevermore.

Upon the ridges of the hills, and also some distance from the encampment both up and down the narrow valley, a double force of sentries was posted. For Saul, with three thousand men, was seeking everywhere for this devoted band; and spies and treacherous friends were many. They were not all of the common rank who were given this sentry duty; for in David's discipline those became captains who were most ready to meet danger and most able to bear hardship and fatigue. So upon this night it fell out that Asahel, brother of one of the chief captains, and himself of high rank among The Thirty, the second order of honor in the band, was stationed at the upper end of the valley. Pacing silently along the dark aisles of the wood, he kept himself unheard, as the darkness kept him unseen. Yet not a sound escaped his trained ear: the stir of the breeze among the

A Man of Valor

branches, the note of the owl or the bulbul, and the distant cry of the prowling dog, were sifted through an ear that listened always for the dangerous sound of a human step.

And the sound came. The crunch of a heel upon a gravelly spot, the crack of a broken twig, declared the near approach of strangers; not one merely, as the sentry's ear told him, nor two, but three or more. He grasped his short, broad-bladed sword, and stood in the path of the intruders. Nearer sounded the steps, nearer, until not more than three paces stood between the unknown comers and the guard. Then in low but sharp tones came his challenge: "In the name of David, stand!"

There was instant silence; for the newcomers, though they must have been expecting to be stopped, seemed wholly taken aback by that sudden challenge, issuing from the darkness but an arm's length before them. Only a moment, however, and a clear, deep voice answered: "'In the name of David!' To see him I am come."

"Who art thou?"

"I am Jonathan," came the answer to the astounded ears of the young Judahite.

Doubting so improbable a thing, and fearing treachery, he kept his sword-arm in guard and his ears alert for any movement, while he said, "If it be indeed thou, my lord, thou wilt pardon a discourtesy for the sake of him thou lovest;" and he whistled a shrill call. In a moment there were sounds of hasty footsteps, and three voices hailed from the darkness close at hand.

"Visitors to our lord, Uriah," said Asahel in somewhat ironical tones. "Lead thou the way. Hezro, keep thou the post."

Then spoke another voice from the front: "If that be Hezro the Carmelite, he knoweth his brother Ben-Ezbai, who hath guided my lord the prince hither."

"Of a truth, Asahel," responded the guard addressed, "it is the voice of Naarai the son of Ezbai, a dweller of the desert, and a friend to our lord."

"We shall see by the eye of the torch," responded the wary Asahel. "Follow, my lord the prince. Ithai, pass with me." And thus, Uriah leading, and the other two closing the rear, the band of six, guarded and guarding, filed toward the camp.

The fires had mostly faded into ashes, but as the file came to the outermost, Uriah, halting the march, stirred the embers into a blaze among some dried rushes, and, dexterously enclosing them in

Uriah stirred the embers into a blaze

some twigs of the oleaster tree, quickly made a torch. Dividing it into two, he passed one to Asahel at the rear, flashing its light, as he passed, upon his charges. The face of the first, now unconcealed by the mantle, looked forth with a frankness, yet a majesty, that abashed the foreign-born soldier; and, though he had never seen the prince Jonathan and had heard only the ambiguous statement of the man Naarai, the thought flashed upon his mind that this must be the king's son, and he whispered to Asahel as he reached him the torch, "It is the prince."

But Asahel, not responding, motioned Uriah to his own place, and strode forward. His own torch he held high above their heads, and gazed earnestly upon the face of the man. Once, several years before, he had seen the prince at Bethlehem, and now he perceived that this was truly he. And though he would scarcely have bowed his haughty knee before his real sovereign, Saul, yet now, before him who was beloved by David's men only less than by David himself, he prostrated himself in a profound obeisance. Rising, he said, with reverence, "My lord Jonathan, David lieth among his men. I lead."

The prince with a gesture stopped at the spot the herdsman Naarai, and, preceded by Asahel and followed by his scout companion Jeziel and by Uriah and Ithai (who, being a native of Gibeah, had also recognized him), he proceeded toward the center camp-fire, that, close to the rocky cliff, was leaping into flame under newly added fuel.

Many recumbent forms, wrapped in mantles, lay about the spot, but one, erect and warrior-like, towered over them all,— the great captain Abishai, whose self-appointed task it had been this night to watch over his master, who never knowingly permitted such care upon the part of his men. As his keen black eyes took in the scene, noting first the graceful form of his brother Asahel, and then the towering, majestic person of his companion, he stooped, waiting for no ceremony, and laid his hand upon the shoulder of his lord. Aroused by the pressure, the leader sprang to his feet, vainly striving, in the moment of awakening, to comprehend with his eye the meaning of the scene before him.

No longer a youth, but a man and a warrior grown, he stood, as the mantle slipped from his shoulders and his eye gained brilliance and keenness, the incarnation of Israel's glory. His golden beard reached his chest, and his hair in light ringlets played about his temples, and, sweeping on, covered his shoulders. Not above average height, and surpassed in stature by nearly all who stood about him, he yet seemed to gather to himself, in his radiant, manly beauty, all the brightness of the scene, and to leave all the gloom to the dark, towering figure of the prince upon the other side of the fire. Yet not all gloom; for the face of Jonathan was lighted with the glow of admiration and love; and, framed in the dark envelope of the night-clad rocks and trees and his own somber mantle and shining black hair, his care-chiseled face was yet so transformed by the fervor of love that in his turn he seemed, rather than to be drawing all light to himself, to be shedding it abroad upon all his dark surroundings. He stood with lips half parted in a smile, waiting for the moment of recognition.

"David!"

"Jonathan! My lord, my brother!" And with the quickness of his own mountain gazelle, the outlaw sprang past the fire into the arms of the law-power, his prince, his friend. They had not met since that fateful day when, from the parting scene in the valley of Gibeah, David had taken his way through Nob, and innocently brought down upon it that awful destruction. And that now, in the wilderness of the hill country, and in the dead of night for fear of detection, his prince should come to visit him and encourage him, to David seemed truly to show the climax of affection. "Thy love to me is wonderful!" he cried now to him in life, as soon he was to cry to him in death.

The warriors, all awakened from sleep, learned by whispers among themselves what had occurred; but, eager though they were to crowd around to pay homage to their prince, the absorption of their two great leaders in each other withheld them, awed them; and gradually in silence they widened their circle and pushed back, leaving the two alone.

Seated before the fire, with their backs to the hillside rock, for hours Jonathan and David remained in converse. What they said none knew; but only as they watched from afar could their followers see, sometimes by the eager gestures, mostly by the animation or depression of their countenances, that they talked of home and loved ones; of the aged Samuel, and the state of piety in the nation; of the affairs of the kingdom, and the danger from the West; of the sorrowful state of the king, and his madness toward David; and of the succession to the throne, which could not long be delayed.

A Man of Valor

The sky was paling in the east when they rose and stood together with clasped hands. "Fear not," were the words of Jonathan to David; "for the hand of Saul my father shall not find thee; and thou shalt be king over Israel, and I shall be next unto thee; and that also Saul my father knoweth." Then again, with right hands clasped and their others uplifted to heaven, they swore together that thrice-bound oath of loyalty one to the other and to their children,— an oath made fuller of meaning now by the birth of the little Mephibosheth.

So they turned and walked toward the bounds of the camp, in the dim gray light of the last morning on which they ever should meet. And now around them came crowding the warriors of David's band, many of whom had served under Jonathan in the wars. They knelt before him; they kissed his hand and the folds of his garments; they prayed aloud for blessings upon him, with David; and they ended in a frenzy of loyal acclaim, by spreading their outer garments under the feet of the advancing princes. Ah, over no such easy path was either to tread to the throne! The way of righteous prince, as of righteous peasant, lies over rough ways and through thorny hedges.

Before they reached the confines of the camp, two well-known figures came to greet them. Gad, a prophet whom Jonathan had seen a number of times in Samuel's school, but who was now by direction of the seer a companion to David, stepped forward to show his fealty and to give his prophet's blessing. With him came one from before whom Jonathan turned away in anguish. There was nothing in his dress to distinguish him from the soldiers around him; yet, had his face been unknown, there was something in the stately movement of his walk that would have proclaimed him a priest. It was Abiathar, sole one of the family of Ahimelech who had escaped from the slaughter at Nob. Here, sheltered with David, he had participated in the hurried marches, the rough life of the camps, and all the hardships of an outlaw's life, yet laboring faithfully with Gad and with David for the uplifting of the desperate characters of many of those who composed the band. He carried with him some of the priest's dress, and was here recognized as the lawful high priest, though Saul had put another in his place. But to meet the son of the man who had murdered his father and all his family, he assumed no part of the distinctive dress which would more fully call to that son's mind his father's crime.

A Man of Valor

All saw the distress of the prince as the lonely high priest, in his rough garb, advanced to meet him, and high in every heart rose a sobbing pity for the man whose father's evil smote his own goodness. The kingship, the priesthood, and the office of prophet were coördinate branches of government in the theocracy of Israel, and priest did not bow to king. Yet, waiving his right, in gentle tones Abiathar said, as he made obeisance, "My lord, receive the homage of one"——

"Nay, Abiathar," interrupted the prince, "bow not to me, who am not your king, and who can not restore the happiness that my house destroyed. But without memory of the past, give, if thou canst, thy blessing to a broken branch of Gibeah's palm." And falling upon his knees, he bowed his royal head before the priest. Affected to tears, as were all who stood by, Abiathar raised his hands above the bowed prince, and pronounced the priestly benediction: —

> The Lord bless thee,
>   And keep thee;
> The Lord make his face to shine upon thee,
>   And be gracious unto thee;
> The Lord lift up his countenance upon thee,
>   And give thee peace.

In the solemn hush that succeeded, the prince

arose, and alone with David passed through the awed and motionless circle, into the wood beyond. There in its depths they parted, and no man saw the parting. But when the sun had risen and cast his beams abroad on the earth, his eye saw upon the road to Hebron a solitary figure, with slow and painful steps making its way back to a restless realm. And upon the high, bare head of a rock-crowned hill hard by Ziph, stood a statue, with hand fixed to brow, over eyes that watched and watched upon the road to Hebron.

CHAPTER VIII

A Night of Gloom

THE West, the fateful West! Rumors from Ekron, a report from Beth-Dagon, alarms from Sharon, word of messengers from Megiddo! The plague of the West had broken out again, and in the defenseless state of the kingdom (defenseless because of the mad demands of the fear-haunted king), town after town had fallen into the hands of the Philistines.

The palace at Gibeah was besieged by terrified refugees, who declared that the might of Achish of Gath was not to be measured by the sands of the sea nor the swelling torrent of Jordan. His chariots of iron stretched in unbroken line from the hills of Gilgal to where the waves of the Great Sea laved their wheel-rims! The glitter of the helmets of his warriors made all the plain a blazing sea of brass! His armies of archers, like dark clouds of vultures, were trooping to the horrible feast of Israel slain! And where in his ivory chariot the proud Philistine king followed his van, there moved with him the exiles of Israel, the desert-hardened, battle-scarred veterans of David of the Hold. Sharon was taken, Baal-shalisha, Pirathon, Gilgal, and Betha; Aner had fallen; Dor was threatened; and, last, the passes of Megiddo had been forced. Jezreel, with all its fair fields and towns, lay at the mercy of the victorious invaders. Where was the Saul of the days of Jabesh-Gilead? Where was Jonathan of Michmash? But ah, fathers! Samuel was dead. But ah, warriors! the lion-banner of Judah was unfurled in the armies of the aliens. Ah, mothers in Israel! blessed were the children that died unborn; for the babes of to-day, like the child of Phineas, must be called Ichabod; for the glory was departed.

Out from the palace gates, out amid the cries of the street, the wailings of a city, strode the fierce captain Abner. Before him with brazen bugles marched the royal trumpeters. Striving with all his will to throw over his countenance an expression of confidence and benignity, he bestowed on the people right and left gnarled smiles of reassurance, here stopping to speak, with rough voice that tried to be smooth, to the frightened child clinging to a disheveled woman's robe; there throwing a look of mingled animation and disdain upon the shrinking forms of men with rent garments and dust-covered heads.

The trumpets began to sound. The alarm of

war, with the stirring martial ring of its intermittent blasts, sounded far over the city and into the camps. At first short, sharp, incisive, they called only to the royal guards. But soon, winding a longer note, they spoke their message to the first levies of the kingdom. A pause, and yet again — lengthened, protracted, persistent — they swelled to the thunder of the full muster-call. The nation was summoned to battle.

Out from the city gates burst first a body of runners, who, separating, turned straightway to north and to south, to east and to west. They were quickly followed by riders upon swift young dromedaries, who should carry the summons to farther points, that Israel's king and Israel's prince and Israel's captain called forth the people to the fight. Let him that bore sword and buckler, let him that drew bow, let him that swung sling, if he be not new builder, if he be not late planter, if he be not but betrothed, if he be not faint-hearted, let him answer the call of the trumpet, and come up to the help of the Lord and of the king.

The night flashed the alarm farther and faster. The beacon-fires flamed up from the rocky cliffs of Benjamin, and leaped to the headlands of Ephraim and Manasseh, Dan, Judah; the mountain-wall of Bashan reflected redly the lurid news, and the shepherds in far Reuben were startled by the sign.

But they stirred not. Muttered the herdsmen of Gad and Reuben, "Has Ammon risen? Let Saul look to his own borders." In Judah it was said, "Let Ephraim now prove his boastings," and, "Where is David?" Dan cowered in the hill fastnesses; for Dan had seen the might of Achish.

With the morning came the muster and the march. Little Benjamin had poured forth its thousands; and, with the king's body-guard as its heart, the Benjamite army, ordered in ranks of five, poured up the valley, defiled through the passage of Michmash, and passed into Ephraim's territory.

The king spoke no word, but with rigid features gazed over the ranks of his tribesmen, and then set his face toward the North. To the energetic Abner he left the details of the army's formation and march.

Behind the king rode his sons Abinadab and Melchishua; by his side, Jonathan. That morning the prince had stood in the midst of his household, and, arrayed in a somber suit of iron mail, newly forged for him, he had bidden a sad farewell. They were few who gathered to speed him. His gentle wife, the mother of his only child, had passed, another Rachel, to the tomb. His servants — the women only, for the men, in the bustle of departure, were busied elsewhere — huddled together at a respectful distance, awed by his changed appearance. Little Mephibosheth, wise with his five years of life, stood forward a little from his nurse, and gazed with archly tilted head to inspect the warrior. But when the father, stepping forward, reached his arms to take him, the child, in sudden fright at the gloomy iron armor, shrank back with a cry into his nurse's arms. In gold and silver and brass he had seen him arrayed before, but what was this black shade of a father, with eyes so dark and awful? He hid his face on his nurse's shoulder.

But then in a moment he heard his father's voice, deep and sweet as when, oh, many, many days ago, it used to call him out to chatter and play among the olives and the vines. He raised his head, and lo, the black cap was gone, and the black eyes were not there; for this was the father of old, with the smiling eyes and the rippling hair and the beautiful curve of the lips. And he was all in the snowy white of a mantle that reached to his feet, and he held his arms out so, as he used to, oh long, so long ago.

And the little master of hearts looked, and turned and looked again, and then into his father's arms he went, and was held so close; and he toyed with the long black beard, that — wasn't it queer? — had gotten streaks of white since the long-ago days, just like the little white lines in the black tents of the desert-dwellers. But, oh, it was a very short time for his father to keep him. And why did the smiling eyes grow black again and become full of tears when he looked up into them? And in a moment his nurse was taking him away, and she was crying, too, and saying over and over, as if she were answering a question, "Yes, I'll keep thee! Yes, I'll keep thee!" But he hadn't asked her if she would keep him. He would rather his father would keep him — or David.

.   .   .   .   .

And so the king rode on, Jonathan by his side. And under the great Standard of the Wolf, and under the ensigns of the families, marched the lion-hearted men of Benjamin. But yet, for all it was a company composed of the kindred of Saul, it held no longer the flower of the army of Israel. It was but a few days or weeks before that the muster would have shown Ahiezer, Joash,

A Man of Valor 171

Pelet, and Berachah, of Gibeah, and Jehu the Antothite, men of renown in the wars, who now it was reported, were to be found with David. There to Ziglag also had fled many of the harried Gibeonites, under their chief Ismaiah, had been alienated by the slaughter of his people. The men of Gedor came with sickness of heart at the loss of their leaders, the sons of Jeroham; and the Korhites—Levites in Benjamin—marched without many a chief already renowned, and yet to become more famous in the wars of David.[6]

The men of Benjamin looked on the face of the king, and it gave no hope. They gazed into the face of Jonathan, and they said, "He looks as one who rides to death." And one answered, " Is it not that David is with the Philistines?" And another said, "My brother is with David." And some said, " Our townsmen Eluzai and Jerimath, are they not also with David?" They said, " Shall we fight our brethren?" And another said, " Will Jonathan fight David?" And again, " If Jonathan fight not, what hope is there for Israel?"

They passed through Ephraim, and came into Manasseh. Ephraim rallied at the king's call, and his bands poured in to swell the force that

[6] See Note 6, Appendix.

must meet for the first time the Philistine on a northern field. And Manasseh mustered his bands, and came to the king's standard. But they looked on the face of the king, and they said, "Is it any more Ebenezer? Is it not Aphek?"[7] That night they pitched their camp by Jezreel, and they saw the Philistines, indeed, in Aphek.

The king leaned on his spear, and stood gazing out through the deepening gloom toward the distant camp of the Philistines. From point to point the torches that marked the divisions of their great army leaped into brightness, and the king saw them extend from Shunem, on the slope of Moreh's hill, north along the base of that solitary ridge, and far out into the plain. The bitterness of a misspent life was carved in his face and his form. Yonder upon the plain lay the avenging hand of God. David, the Chosen, whom he had sought to slay, was there. To-morrow ——?

He had no word from God. His inquiries through the priest brought no reply: he had slain the priests. His appeal for a message through the prophets was answered not: the prophets had broken with him. His desperate endeavors to bring on visions in his sleep were of no avail: his dreams were only of the horrible and the gro-

---
[7] See Note 7, Appendix.

A Man of Valor

tesque; they were not from God. Like the dank horror of the darkness in this unlighted camp of Israel was the despair that brooded over his soul — with the hoarse whisper of the demon winds that swept over gray Gilboa; with the ghastly swish of the deep-musing, pale waters — the fountain of Jezreel, the well of Harod, "the waters of trembling;" with the cold, unblinking stars looking down upon all, unmoved by man's passion and untouched by his woe.

He was the anointed of God; he was the rejected of God. He could not meet that terrible enemy to-morrow without some message from heaven. He was the anointed of God: was there not another anointed? He had heard that Samuel had anointed that other. And long ago it was Samuel who had said to him, "The Lord hath rent the kingdom of Israel from thee this day, and hath given it to a neighbor of thine, that is better than thou." And the day had come. To-morrow was David's day, the day of his revenge. He would come in with the Philistines; he would take his crown from the hand of the uncircumcised.

At that the pride of the Hebrew, the pride of the Benjamite, surged through the veins of the king. He had ever fought the enemy of his people; he would never stoop to ask the aid of

Gath. And Samuel, though Samuel was dead,— would Samuel sanction this dastardly course of his new choice, this *better* neighbor? Oh, if he could only see Samuel! Would that it were true, as all but Israel, and many in Israel, believed, that the dead were not dead, that from the world of Sheol they watched over the affairs of the living still. Then would Samuel help him; for Samuel had been his friend. But the priest could get for him no answer; the prophets shunned him; in his dreams he saw only the spirits of devils. What then! were there none who could stand between the living and the dead, who could open the mysteries of the world of spirits? Of all the necromancers and diviners who had infested the land, and whom, in his seeking for merit, he had slain according to the law, was there not left one? For such an one — such an one — could such an one bring up Samuel?

.   .   .   .   .

The camp of Israel was on the spot where, two hundred years before, the army of Gideon had lain when the Midianites and the Amalekites and all the dwellers of the desert had pitched in the plain. Jonathan, musing not only upon his own life, but upon the dealings of God with his people in all times past, recalled the history of that won-

A Man of Valor

derful deliverance through the man of Manasseh: the faint-hearted muster, the dwindling of the host, the trial that gave the fountain its ancient name, and the consequent selection of the Three Hundred; then the strategem that confounded their innumerable enemies, and gave victory to Israel. A few miles beyond lay Tabor, where Barak had encamped just before his battle with the Canaanites, the might of whose iron chariots was turned into confusion in the miry plain when the Lord fought with the weapons of the cloud.

But now there was no Deborah to give encouragement; no angel had appeared with a commission from heaven. Instead, there was a king who listened for prophets' voices and heard demons', and who would fain have wrung ten thousand fleeces could he have found one drop of dew. And he, Jonathan, was bound upon the morrow to lead into combat men who saw the handwriting of defeat on one another's faces; who knew that their best and bravest had deserted to David; whose forlorn hope of victory lay only in him, their prince. And he must lead them — hillsmen, foot-soldiers — into battle on a chariot-swept plain, in the face of tremendous odds of numbers; yes, even against some of their own countrymen and kindred, and against David.

And this he must do because he was the prince of Israel, because his father was Saul. For Saul he had fought from his youth; for God and for Saul at Jabesh-Gilead, at Geba, at Michmash; for Israel and for Saul in the desert, in Ammon, in Zobah, in Philistia; for Saul he would now fight at the close of his life — not for Israel, for the heart of Israel was David; not for God, for God was not with this army. Yet, too, he fought for God: that he fought for Saul was at the behest of God, who said, "Honor thy father." Yet, too, he fought for Israel; for yonder host, though allied with David, was the enemy of Israel.

And would David, the anointed of God, fight against the people of God? True, he had been persecuted, hunted, exiled, by Saul; but, though seemingly forced to live in dependence upon the king of the Philistines, he had never raised his hand against his own people. And now that he was in the hostile ranks, it must be by force. For David loved Israel; David loved him. He would have given the throne long before to David, but God had not opened the way. He would have stood below the throne and upheld David; but now he knew he should not be there to hail the coronation. But David, he knew, would not

A Man of Valor

seek the throne over the bloody corpses of his countrymen. God was good: he would not suffer his anointed one to do that wrong.

Yes, God was good. In the councils of heaven there had been a discordant spirit who sought the hurt of them that feared God and forsook evil; and many had been the trials that the righteous had borne. Pain and loss, suspicion and scorn, these had been touches of the finger of God; but the Voice had said, "Upon himself put not forth thine hand." And somewhere in the trials had been hidden a purpose of God. "When He hath tried me, I shall come forth as gold." And if it be to death, "All the days of my appointed time will I wait, till my change come. Thou shalt call, and I will answer thee: thou wilt have a desire to the work of thine hands."

Over all the blur of the evil past there swept a purging hand, and through the white page ran a golden thread, the purpose of God with him. Clear now was all the course that without sight he had run. Tyranny had been missed through toil; ambition had been checked by humiliation; glory had been subjected by shame; generosity had been fostered by a noble friendship; love had been purified by the resisted assaults of self-interest. Now he yielded again his life, his strange, his barren life (nay, but the angels said, his fruitful life), into the hands of his God, who had given and kept it. The peace of God came down upon him, and the warfare of a life was ended.

The night was chill, and white vapors, rising from the streams behind Gilboa, began to roll down upon the encampment at its foot. Dimly the belated lights of the army's divisions bleared through the white darkness. As the prince rose and turned toward his tent, there brushed by him three muffled forms, with faces set toward Shunem, and he heard the muttered word, "Endor!" The voice, the form, to one who had passed a life-time of intimacy with them, proclaimed the king.

· · · · ·

In the camp of Manasseh there were great searchings of heart. This was hallowed ground to Manasseh; but this was not a hallowed nor a hopeful cause. And many were they who argued: "God has forsaken our king. Samuel anointed David king. Shall we fight against David?" And some answered: "Shall David fight against Israel? Is that the work of its king? Who will desert Jonathan? and who God? For if God hath deserted Saul, Jonathan he hath not left." "But certain it is," said they all,

A Man of Valor

"that to-morrow will see no victory for Saul; for the hope of God hath left his face."

"But Jonathan! Will not God fight with Jonathan?"

"The soul of Jonathan is knit with the soul of David. Jonathan will not fight."

"Nay; let it not be thought that Jonathan comes to battle, and not to fight!"

"But if it be as at Ephes-dammim? There none fought till David came."

"It is not Ephes-dammim; for here Issachar, Zebulon, Asher, and Naphtali lie at the feet of Achish, and the caravans of the North fall prey to him, while the fields of Jezreel are eaten up. Saul must fight."

At that came into the council of the captains, Elihu, one of their number. "Men of Manasseh," he cried, "the son of Jesse is not with the Philistines. He departs this night for Ziglag."

"How knowest thou that?" came a chorus of voices.

"By the word of one of his band, Jeziel of Gibeah, well known to me, who hath come from David to declare it."

"Then may we fight," cried some. "Let it be told our lord Jonathan."

But amid the general acclamation, six of the

circle sat silent, sunk suddenly in thought. And when the council broke up, and each went his way, these, finding Elihu, spoke a plan, to which he silently, and with sadness, assented.

· · · · ·

Carmel's heights were yet untouched by the rosy light of the morning, and the heavy dew of the night had not shaken one pearly drop from tip to root, when from behind the fortifications of the entrained chariots at Shunem, emerged a band six hundred strong, that ghost-like moved rapidly and silently across the plain toward the hills of Megiddo. And at the same time, from the southern camp at the fountain of Jezreel, a smaller band stole secretly away, gathering in as it went the sentries on that side — six sentries who bore rank as captains in the thousands of Manasseh.

As they passed out of sight over the rolling hills of the plain, on the way that led to Megiddo, from the direction of Endor came three men, the middle one of towering form, but now shrunken and bent, the two upon his either side supporting him with their arms. They came to the sentries' posts, and the two marveled that the camp lay open without guards; but the king, with unseeing eyes, stared straight upon the stony heights of Gilboa, as if he saw a grim and cruel vision.

CHAPTER IX

Gilboa

MANY a carnage have the hills seen that cluster around the great triangle of the plain of Jezreel, or Esdraelon; yet at but one other time have they beheld so terrible an overthrow of an army that fought in the name of God, as on the black day of Gilboa. Shut within the narrow limits set by Gilboa and Little Hermon (then called Moreh), the armies of Philistia and of Israel marshaled themselves for battle.

It was not a field such as an Israelite would have chosen. Unsupplied with chariots, wholly unskilled in their use, and practically without cavalry, the Hebrew warriors fought mostly on foot, and, when the choice lay with them, selected the hills and the passes for the field of combat. But here the invading force held too fair and fruitful a tract, and threatened too insupportable a damage, to allow of inactivity on the part of Israel's king. Jezreel must be wrested from the grasp of the Philistine, and he be sent in rout through the passes by which he had come, if military prestige and national power were to be preserved.

Twice before, indeed, had Israel, on this and on a near-by field, wrung glorious victories from her foes upon such unequal terms. But Barak had attacked and triumphed at a moment when furious storms had sodden the ground and swelled the torrents, to the discomfiture of Sisera's horsemen; and Gideon had won by strategem against an unorganized and excitable foe. Then God was with the leaders, and he both planned and worked for his people. Now the enemy was the most steady and valorous of the peoples of Syria; no night was to mask a possible surprise; and God spoke no word of encouragement, nor promised any succor. On the chosen field of their foes the Israelite army must make its desperate assault against ranks bristling with spears, from behind which archers in safety discharged their clouds of arrows, and from whose flanks issued squadrons of chariots that, charging through the files, dealt unassailable death along their wide-streaked paths.

From the green sea of the fruitful plains the mountain range of Gilboa rose gray and forbidding. Its lower slopes, upon the last of which Saul's army lay partly encamped, swelled in not unpleasing prospect to the line of its sheer cliffs, that in their gray whiteness seemed now, even to the hill-loving Israelite, to menace rather than to

A Man of Valor

offer aid. Thus stood Gilboa, revealing, as the eye ran up its form, no evidence of dew, nor rain, neither "fields of offerings,"— stood a stern and unpitying spectator of the tragedy that day should bring forth.

Two or three miles across the upward sloping plain, with Little Hermon as a background, the Philistine army stood in bright and dread array. The resources of the five-headed nation had been strained to gather this great host, which King Achish intended should settle finally the long-contested struggle between Philistia and Israel. None who could bear arms were excused. It was due to this imperative call that David and his men had been found in the ranks of the Philistine army. Only upon the angry protestations of the Philistine lords, who feared he might, at some critical stage of the battle, deliver his band into the hands of Israel's king, had Achish finally, with reluctance, been forced to dismiss him.

Though important enough because of their valor, the men of David were few in number, and their absence caused no apparent diminution of the power of King Achish. With horsemen and chariots, with spearmen and archers, with heavily armored men of war who handled sword and shield, and with a band of the terrible Anakim as its heart and tower of strength, the Philistine army stood forth, glittering in gold, and silver, and brass, and iron; proud, confident, and seemingly invincible.

On the other hand, the army of Israel, accoutered, indeed, in far better manner than when first Saul had seen them in battle array, were nevertheless inferior in equipment and in numbers, while the very confidence of their foes increased the despondency which the appearance of their king and the conditions of the time had induced. Yet they were by no means a despicable force. Their levies were from three of the four greatest fighting tribes of the nation; their archers, though less numerous, were not less skilful than the Philistines'; their foot-soldiers, at least in the hills, which they trod most confidently, were not surpassed in skill and courage by any foreigners; and their redoubtable slingers, who "could sling stones at a hair's-breadth, and not miss," more terrible in their powers of execution than archers or dart-slingers, were in distant battle-fare not to be rivaled by any branch of service in the opposing army. Though weakened by skulking and desertion, and by the recent alienation and self-banishment of some of its greatest leaders, the Israelite army, so efficient had been its training under the monarchy, was yet powerful and formidable.

A Man of Valor

Thus stood arrayed the two armies of these most mortal foes. The morning had advanced not a little before the disposition of the Hebrew troops had been completed; while the Philistine soldiers, determined to maintain their advantage of an open plain, rested upon their arms in expectation of the assault.

Spent with toil and grief and horror, Saul had reëntered his camp in the early morning, palsied in mind and body. The last hope had been driven from his heart: by the Wrecker of souls, impersonating the one in whom he trusted, he had been foretold of his ruin — not only that he himself should die, but that with him his house should perish, and Israel fall. "To-morrow," had declared the suppositious Samuel, "shalt thou and thy sons be with me; the Lord also shall deliver the host of Israel into the hand of the Philistines." Of his four legitimate sons, one, true, was not present in the army; but on him, whose very name was "Man of Shame,"— indolent, voluptuous, pusillanimous,— the king counted nothing; and his only descendant of the second generation was the infant Mephibosheth. Truly, the way was open for David.

But of despair was born a desperate courage. Shut within his pavilion, Saul composed his mind and nerved his heart to command and to fight as a king, to fall as a hero. He came forth with a visage washed from the stains of the night's anguish, and set about the ordering of the battle. As he proceeded, he gained more and more animation and assurance. His eyes sparkled; his voice took on the old-time martial ring; and his whole bearing became that of a confident leader.

When the sun's beams had chased the shadows of the eastern hills down from the summits of Gilboa, and, flooding first the western plains, had bathed at last the fountain of Jezreel, the Israelite army stood in completed battle-array upon the plain. The host was marshaled in three divisions, right, center, and left, under the standards of Ephraim, Benjamin, and Manasseh. There were, first, the heavy-armed troops, the spearmen, who were armed also with swords, and, besides wearing complete body-armor, bore upon their left arms the long triangular shield. Ten deep in rank and in file, they were thus made into divisions of one hundred, ten of such divisions making the thousand. Upon the march, they went only five men abreast, every alternate file having dropped to the rear. Each file had its captain, as had the higher divisions, these making the "captains of tens and of fifties and of hundreds and of thousands."

Spread out in the field in front of this body were ranged in open order the archers and the slingers, who sometimes bore also several javelins, or light spears, for throwing. These troops, being intended not so much for hand-to-hand fighting as for distant offensive work, wore neither armor nor weapons so complete as those of the spearmen. Their shields were light, round bucklers, made of tough oxhide stretched upon wooden frames, or of wickerwork; and their body-armor, so much of it as they wore, was at this time more often of leather than of anything heavier. Yet they also carried short, broad, two-edged swords.

The center division was ranged under the command of the king himself; while Abner, upon the right, commanded the Ephraimites, and Jonathan, with his noblest brother, Abinadab, and a few Benjamite slingers, was over the Manassites, upon the left. Upon heavily mailed horses the three commanders sat just to the rear of the lines, from which position in the battle they might discover the needs of any part of their division, and send aid.

With their faces set upon the distant hostile array, the men of Israel stood, waiting for the customary oration and announcements, and the signal for combat. Distributed among the different divisions, the Korhites stood with silver trumpets in readiness to blow. With the company by the king stood also priests, from whose lips was first to come the signal, at the command of the king. Suddenly, clear and high in the still air rose the ringing notes of the trumpet, caught up and echoed along the ranks from center to wings. As the last notes died away, the soldiers' expectant eyes were turned upon three priests of the family of Zadok, one before each army division, who, in the pontifical robes of snowy white, stepped out before the line, and, in clear, resonant voices spoke the battle exhortation: —

"Hear, O Israel, ye approach this day unto battle against your enemies; let not your hearts faint, fear not, and do not tremble, neither be thou terrified because of them; for the Lord your God is he that goeth with you, to fight for you against your enemies, to save you."

As at the center, in the king's presence, the priest's voice dwelt upon the words, "For the Lord your God is he that goeth with you, to fight for you against your enemies, to save you," Saul's cheek went pale, and he shuddered with his knowledge of the present falsity of the words which had so many times before encouraged him. But with a strong effort recovering his composure, he fixed his courage and fired his heart to go down, like

A Man of Valor

Samson, with a greater revenge than his life had ever given.

As the priests retired, from the ranks stepped before each thousand its captain, and, to the subdued accompaniment of trumpets, recited in concert the formal charge: —

"What man is there that hath built a new house, and hath not dedicated it? let him go and return to his house, lest he die in the battle, and another man dedicate it.

"And what man is he that hath planted a vineyard, and hath not yet eaten of it? let him also go and return unto his house, lest he die in the battle, and another man eat of it.

"And what man is there that hath betrothed a wife, and hath not taken her? let him go and return unto his house, lest he die in the battle, and another man take her."

Then, after a pause,—

"What man is there that is fearful and faint-hearted? let him go and return unto his house, lest his brethren's heart faint as well as his heart."

Not a man stirred from the ranks. Then, louder, shriller, full of defiance, blared the trumpets. They ceased suddenly, and there rose a hoarse, terrific shout, with the clangor of swords against shields. As it died away, the trumpets gave one long, clear blast, and the ranks moved forward, slowly at first, with firm tread, to the music of the battle-chant. It was an anthem of the recent wars,—so strangely sung here,—a song learned of David when he was captain of the host; a song that contained a response from the king, but intoned for him by a company of singing priests: —

The People

Jehovah answer thee in the day of trouble;
> The name of the God of Jacob set thee up on high,

Send thee help from the sanctuary,
> And strengthen thee out of his holy hill,

Remember all thy offerings,
> And accept thy burnt-offerings,

Grant thee thy heart's desire,
> And fulfil all thy counsel.

We will triumph in thy victory,
And in the name of our God we will set up our banners:
> Jehovah fulfil all thy petitions.

The King

Now know I that Jehovah saveth his anointed:
He will answer him from his holy heaven
With the saving strength of his right hand.

The People

Some trust in chariots, and some in horses,
> But we will make mention of the name of Jehovah, our God.

They are bowed down and fallen,
> But we are risen and stand upright.

O Lord, save the king!
> And answer us when we call.

A Man of Valor

As the Israelite army moved forward to the attack, there was animation in the ranks of the Philistines. Their trumpets answered defiance with defiance, and shortly they also were in motion toward the center of the plain. Far extended were their glittering ranks, overlapping by several furlongs the opposing lines of the Hebrews, especially upon the left, where the broad plain made the maneuvering of their chariots most favorable. To meet the threatened outflanking, the Hebrew prince extended his line by defiling some of the hinder ranks to the left, of necessity weakening thereby the strength of the deep formation.

In the center King Achish opposed himself to Saul, having put his wings under the charge of different lords of the cities of Philistia. Behind the shield of his heavily armed spearmen, and surrounded by his archers and his huge Anakim guard, he rode in an ivory-covered chariot after four milk-white, iron-armored steeds abreast, himself arrayed in armor of the finest forged iron, inlaid with gold. With him in the car were his charioteer, a man of high rank, who handled the reins; and also a third person, his shield-bearer. All three, if they became involved in the *mêlèe,* fought with sword and bow, the charioteer wrapping the reins around his waist, and guiding his horses with a touch of the hand or a contortion of the body.

Behind the king followed, at a little distance, a squadron of chariots in loose formation; and others were ranged at intervals along the whole rear line. Their equipment was similar to that of the king, though, being smaller, they each were drawn by but two horses, and contained only two occupants. Above their iron sides protruded the bow-cases and the quivers filled with arrows. From each axle extended a sharp, scythe-like blade, several feet long, capable of doing awful execution when the chariot was in rapid motion.

At last the forces joined battle. As they drew within bowshot, the air became darkened with the clouds of arrows. At first the distance was too great for them to do great execution, but as the space between narrowed, their force became greater, and many a shield was pierced, and many an armor-joint was found. With them shortly came a hail of stones, many of several pounds' weight, and cast with a force that crushed brazen helmets and shattered iron shields. The cries of the combatants grew fiercer and more terrific. At last, when the opposing lines were separated by no more than half a furlong, the trumpets gave one final signal, the archers and slingers retired

A Man of Valor

between opening files that quickly closed again, and the spearmen charged upon their foes. Thrust and counter, lunge and ward, sally and assault, while the thunder of the granite hail dinned a reverberant undertone, and the swift storm of arrows let the light beat in as through the playing shuttles of a mighty loom.

The shouts died down, for breath was precious; but the uproar sank not for that. The clangor of iron against iron, the creak of armor twisted in the death grapple, the neighing and squealing of the war-horses that champed and stamped in eager inactivity, the curses of the wounded, and the shrieks of the mortally stricken, rose like a hoarse cacophony from Gehenna's pit, yet dominated by the measured, deep-toned voices of the commanders giving orders, and by the clarion signals of the trumpets.

Hundreds of men went down along that gory furrow, yet neither side would yield a cubit's space, save to find new ground for footing, as the field became piled with the corpses of the slain.

Where Jonathan fought, with Manasseh, the fish-bodied standard of Dagon marked the presence of the Ashdodites on the left, while the array of Ashkelon stretched between them and the Gittites in the center. The Manassites were not behind the men of Benjamin in joining battle, nor was the fight less deadly. But here the Philistines, being in greater number, sought constantly to outflank their foes; and when the Israelite line of battle was weakened by deploying to the left to meet the threatening movement, the Philistines sought the harder to break through. But one of eagle eye and strong arm withstood them. It mattered not that seven of their mightiest captains and many men had deserted overnight, the Manassites, feeling themselves under the eye of Jonathan, who had seen Jabesh-Gilead and Geba and Michmash, and many another glorious field, acquitted themselves like men, and maintained a steady and aggressive front toward the enemy.

Wherever danger was greatest, there was Jonathan. Where the hostile charge sought to break through the thin line, there his animating voice and his strong arm would restore the quailing and urge on the bold. Where a concentered storm of arrows sought to open a gap for the Philistine spearmen, there he braved it in the thickest, while his slingers and bowmen overwhelmed with their missiles the hostile archers. Despite the odds against them, the men of Manasseh steadily pressed back the heathen hosts cubit by cubit.

So far the chariot force of the Philistines had

been given no chance to engage. Now the princes of Ashdod and Ashkelon, unable to make headway in front, prepared to launch a blow from this most dreaded arm. The prince of Israel saw the beginning of the maneuver, and, to the best of his power, prepared to meet it. The attack would come in flank. Withdrawing from his already weak line some of his most courageous spearmen, he stretched them in wide-strung order, extending from his rear toward Gilboa. In advance of these he set first a company of archers, then his band of Benjamite slingers, and behind he placed in denser formation a triple line of spearmen.

The battle had been in progress some hours, and for very weariness the combatants had slackened the ardor of the fight along the most of the battle-front, their attention being chained to the hazard of the separate affrays which various of the opposing captains, more tireless than their followers, and covetous of glory, still maintained. Compared with the previous turmoil, there reigned now a quiet, ominous indeed to the few who saw the bolt being forged.

The archers upon the newly formed front, behind the outmost wing of the army, had been given their posts, and were receiving the final directions and exhortations of their prince, when a noise as of the rumbling of distant thunder made every heart leap and every eye grow anxiously alert: it was the sound of the chariot charge.

All at once the Philistine host resumed the offensive, pressing with fierce cries and fiercer blows upon their enemies. Over the heads of the spearmen, a hundred paces to the rear, could be seen the edge of the chariot wave, three cars in depth, racing to the left. Widening the space between the lines as they neared the end, they began a wide sweeping turn, so timed that as they swung around the flank, each line joined its extreme end to the inner of the line in advance, and they faced for the charge sixscore chariots abreast.

On they came, a furious, raging, animate avalanche — through the dust-clouds' rolling folds swift pictures of leaping horses, jumping chariots, drivers urging on with voice and lash. The Israelites upon the exposed flank could not stand before this awful certainty of death and disaster, and began hastily to retire. The Philistine footmen, pressing on more furiously, threatened to turn already the retirement into a rout; but the Israelite prince, riding up, incited his men to fight more valiantly, while he swiftly bent the line around into a bow, thus drawing the eagerly pursuing Philistine spearmen between the Hebrews

On they came, a furious, raging, animate avalanche

and their own charging chariots. Their rapid retreat brought the retiring warriors within the newly formed battle-front, while the skilful maneuver broke and shortened the line of chariots.

Already the arrows were flying, and Jonathan, speeding along behind his company of archers, by word and gesture encouraged them in their last effort. With a final volley, the bowmen turned and fled behind the slingers. These Benjamites, few in number, but mighty in deed, were now the hope of the Israelites. Instantly, clear from the bowmen, they let fly their missiles.

Dexterous as those chariot-warriors were, maintaining perfect poise in their bounding, swaying cars, and dodging or catching upon their shields the shafts aimed at them, they were not equal to the task of evading the aim of the Benjamite slingers. Leaden bullets, swift and unseen, found no interposed targets, and the hail of the heavier stones was too fierce to be wholly warded off. Charioteer, pitching forward, threw loose the reins; smitten warrior sank on lifeless limbs; chariots swerved and plunged madly into one another. Yet still the charge, blocked only here and there, came on. In their turn the slingers followed the bowmen through the opening ranks of their friends; yet some, bolder or tardier than the rest, drew sword, and sought an unequal fight where Jonathan led, amid thundering hoofs and wheels and whizzing knives.

As the slingers melted away, the first rank of spearmen stood to meet the onset. They were meant to be sacrificed, but to save. Their heavy spears leveled at the armored breasts of the horses, they braced themselves for a shock no men could stand. Behind their splintered spears the whole line went down beneath the hoofs and the wheels; but they saved the hour. Shattered and broken, the chariot wave surged unevenly on against the solid shield wall that yet confronted them.

The force of the charge was gone, and in stationary fight the few chariot-warriors could not maintain themselves against their numerous and well-armed opponents. Traces were cut, horses hewed down; and, to add to the disaster, some of the steeds, left masterless by the slingers, were caught by the daring Benjamites and turned against their fellows. It needed no skilled hands to direct those war engines into bloody fields. The frenzied horses plunged, with the foreign-manned cars, along the rear of the Philistine chariots, following that mounted sable leader, whose arrows flew swift and certain as the thunderbolts and hail that ancient Egypt saw.

The Philistines had poured forth a supporting column of footmen behind the chariots, but so sudden and effective had been the blocking of the way that, before these could reach the spot, it became a question whether even one chariot could be saved to the men of the plain. With desperate endeavors, a few disengaged themselves, and turned their backs upon their enemies. Plunging back over the way they had come, they charged upon their friends, who, however, mostly succeeded in opening ranks and letting them pass through without giving damage, shamed and humiliated by a defeat from foot-soldiers. For perhaps only the third time in the history of Israel, a chariot charge on a plain had been met and repulsed.

The new battle-line thus formed, in shape like a bow, was maintained with desperate courage by the Manassites, who feared and fought the evident purpose of the enemy to cut off their retreat to the hills, and hem them in upon the plain. Again the battle raged, as at the first, between spear and shield, sword and helm.

Then came the great disaster. In the center, under the eyes of their respective kings, Benjamites and Gittites stubbornly contested the ground. Here the Israelites, there the Philistines, gave way a space, as valor or strength found itself mismatched. So the line became broken and irregular. Just in front of King Saul, his boldest and mightiest had pushed back the Philistine front, and were hewing their way through to the eagle-headed standard of Achish. The Hebrew slingers had, by Saul's order, begun to concentrate their attack upon the Gittite king; but he, gathering around him his giant guard of ten, made of their shields a sheltering wall. Yet some of the missiles of his foemen reached or pierced through, and his high-mettled steeds, already restive, became almost unmanageable under the bombardment. He must either retire or change the fortune of the field.

The bold band that were cleaving their way through the Philistine lines were becoming separated from their comrades, and in their wedge formation exposed their flanks. Directing his fighters to fall back suddenly, Achish poured a torrent of arrows from the bows of his archers upon the opposing front. Then, opening his ranks in the center, he launched half his Anakim guard upon the head of the Israelite column. Before these terrible fighting-machines, man after man went down; and though, assailed by three desperate Benjamites, one fell not to rise again, the rest forged still on toward King Saul.

A Man of Valor 201

Still the Benjamites did not lose courage, but closed in behind their mighty foes, hemming them in and assailing them from rear as well as front. But now some, with the turning of their backs, exposed themselves to the ceaseless flight of arrows, and, moreover, by their confusion in rank, gave Achish the opportunity for which he had planned. Opening his ranks yet more, he signaled his chariot force, and himself led the furious charge. Entering where the shield wall was broken, he opened a gap that his other chariots, following, rent still wider.

At once the field became a scene of greater carnage. Though King Saul, with ringing voice, strove to rally his men, and himself wrought deeds of wonder with sword and mace, it availed little. The slingers and archers, seeing the chariots charging, deserted their ground and ran for the hills; and the spearmen, half fighting, half flying, became quickly demoralized. Wedged in the thick masses which as yet could find no clearance, they could only half resist, and, their courage gone, they threw away their discipline.

The panic spread. The wedge-formed chariot charge was extending ever wider its wings. The Benjamite division, cleft in the center, was crumpled back in helpless masses upon either side, that shortly found themselves back to back with Manasseh or driving down the rear of Ephraim.

In the midst of the fight and rout, Saul strove with desperate valor still to block the progress of his victorious foe. With his son Melchishua at his side, he fought at the forefront, and all the fiercer as he saw the fulfilment of his expected doom. Hundreds of his foemen felt the edge of his blade that day, and in his raging battle-ire he looked to them a very god; for their gods were demons. But his men were flying; his battalia was gone; he had lost the field. In valiant combat his son fell in death before his eyes; his armor-bearer and a few of his guards alone supported him as they reached the slopes of Gilboa, and, backward fighting, crept up its heights.

On either side the ground was not long maintained. The haughty-hearted Ephraimites, who had all day sought, not to emulate, but to set an example for their brethren of Benjamin and Manasseh, now gave way before the assaults of the victorious Philistines with foot and horse and chariot; and, with Abner, their commander, they were swept down the valley in ever increasing confusion and loss.

The Manassites, desperately holding their own

behind the barrier they had made of the bodies of men and beasts, were brought with sudden shock to a knowledge of their danger, when the disorganized mass of Benjamites came pressing in upon their rear. The Philistines, in charge upon charge, were driving them ever closer; and if the way to the hills of Gilboa should be taken, the Hebrews would be at the mercy of foes who gave no quarter. Retreat must be instant.

While he should strive to reform and save the bands of Benjamin, Jonathan directed his brother Abinadab to bring off the Manassites. It was no easy task. The movement must be in column, fighting on the side and rear. When the Ashdodites and men of Ashkelon saw the long-contested field being abandoned by their foes, they pressed on in exultation, striving at the same time to cast a force ahead of them, to block their path. The battle quickly became a race. Ranks were broken, discipline was ignored.

Again the chariots charged, and the horrors of the middle field became those of the left. In rout and ruin, Manasseh was swept back upon Jezreel. Captains became privates, fighting for life. Bands were broken; standards were lost. Only a few retained the valor that is the heritage of princely souls.

In vain Jonathan sought to stay the rout, to stop the slaughter. Israel was perishing before his eyes; and, but for the deeds his own hand wrought, there shortly came to be nothing done to save them. The most valiant of his friends went down. As they were swept past the fountain and through their camp upon the lower slopes of Gilboa, he saw his valiant brother, standing before the royal pavilion, receive the onset of a dozen swordsmen, and fall at last from the arrows of his more distant foes.

Israel was dying. Benjamin lay upon the plain below. Ephraim was flying in rout down the valley. Manasseh was scattered upon the hills as sheep stampeded by wolves, flying, not fighting. The remnant of Benjamin that, with the king, reached the rocky mountainside, maintained for a time a disorganized and futile contest with their tenacious pursuers; but their familiar hill-lands gave them now no confidence. Their foes were flushed with victory and great in numbers. They pressed the fugitives hard, and their archers, at every irresolute stand the Hebrews made, reaped a harvest of death with their shafts. The day grew old with slaughter, and the sinking sun above Carmel cast his red eye upon a king who stood at bay behind a heap

The dim eyes of the prince enclosed beneath a darkening sky

A Man of Valor

of slain, bleeding, fainting, sinking, under the iron hail that Philistine archers from afar poured in upon him.

Upon the heights above the fountain of Jezreel, Jonathan had made his last stand. They were few, but they were dear, who stood with him in that hour of unutterable woe. Encircling their beloved commander, those great hearts of Benjamin held their own in brotherhood to the last. Their whirring slings called death; their bowstrings, twanging, sang a refrain of the mighty in the midst of the battle; their swords marked out a boundary that none sought to pass. Valiant as the lion of their native hills, they fell as the lion falls, ringed round by quaking hunters. And the chase swept on where the fying led the way.

. . . . .

The dim eyes of the prince unclosed beneath a darkening sky. The sun had set, and the shroud of the night was falling upon the bier of Israel. Alone, one brilliant star, low down in the east, had set its watch for the sleeping. Around the stricken field, the ancient hills of Israel kept still their silent guard: the land of God stood firm; his people alone might perish. Beyond these heights the rolling hills led down the green uplands of Ephraim to Benjamin's crags and gorges. There Gibeah waited, and should wait in vain, to welcome a conqueror as of old. For the messengers that should be, would come with flying feet, with garments rent, and dust upon their heads, and the wail of a nation should find its voice in Gibeah. The palace doors should keep no guard, and the doom of the father should be told in the ears of the child. Little one, little one, that knowest naught of the guilt of thy house; little hands, that have played with the sunbeams and never toyed with the bow; eyes of the trustful, wells of the love of Rachel — ah, little one, who shall stand for thee now? No arms of a warrior shield thee, but frail, frail arms of a timid heart; for the frightened fly, and the Jordan is far. Thou art in the arms of thy nurse,— sheltering arms, if they drop thee not, if they drop thee not.

The rocks of Benjamin fade away; and far in the South, where the desert sweeps in to the green-fringed wells, the standard of Judah is raised over a band with sleepless swords. David, in thee shall the weak be strong; for thou, the anointed of the Lord, shalt break with Philistia, and bury Gilboa upon the plains of Gath. And when the time shall come that Jehovah giveth

A Man of Valor

thee rest from all thine enemies round about, then above the sword shall the harp be raised, and that glorious voice shall chant the triumph of Israel.

A voice? Was it a voice from the battle-field, from the stricken, the dying, a voice that raised the old, old song of "The Lord Our Rock"? Nay; the hand of death was closing the heavy eyes, and the ear alike was touched and sealed from earthly sounds. The voice was the voice of the harper of Bethlehem in the palace halls of Gibeah long ago: —

> Give ear, ye heavens, and I will speak;
>   And let the earth hear the words of my mouth:
> My doctrine shall drop as the rain,
>   My speech shall distil as the dew,
> As the small rain upon the tender grass,
>   And as the showers upon the herb.
> For I will proclaim the name of Jehovah:
>   Ascribe ye greatness unto our God.
> The Rock, his work is perfect;
>   For all his ways are judgment:
> A God of faithfulness and without iniquity,
>   Just and right is he.

The Lord is just; his ways are right —" visiting the iniquity of the fathers upon the children unto the third and fourth generation "— the third generation! and if thy keeper drop thee not, Mephibosheth; for the Jordan is far —

> For Jehovah's portion is his people,
>   Jacob is the lot of his inheritance.
> He found him in a desert land,
>   And in the waste howling wilderness.
> He compassed him about, he cared for him;
>   He kept him as the apple of his eye.
> As an eagle that stirreth up her nest,
>   That fluttereth over her young,
> He spread abroad his wings, he took them,
>   He bare them on his pinions:
> Jehovah alone did lead him.—

He holdeth the hand of his anointed; and as a shepherd leadeth his flock, so, David, shall thy steps be led. Remember; forget not: "Thou shalt not cut off thy kindness from my house forever; no, not when the Lord hath cut off the enemies of David every one from the face of the earth." "While I yet live — while I yet live, show me the kindness, the loving-kindness of the Lord, that I die — that I die —

> There is none like unto God, O Jeshurun,
>   Who rideth upon the heavens for thy help,
>   And in his excellency on the sky.
> The eternal God is thy refuge,
>   And underneath are the everlasting arms.

The eyes were closed, the ears were stopped, the voice died away; but the sinking spirit, as it gave itself to God, felt underneath the Everlasting Arms.

CHAPTER X

The Song of the Bow

AROUND the blackened ruins of a fire-smitten city in southern Philistia a great encampment lay spread out. Black tents of the desert and those of the gayer northern weave were pitched in the midst of heaps of spoil: furniture for tents and for riding-animals, war weapons, gold and silver ornaments, and garments. Round about the encampment were droves of camels and asses and white-fleeced flocks, watched over by boys with slings. Within and among the tents, women and children were mingling in chattering groups, or busied with tasks, some at work upon rent garments, some sitting before the flat stone mills, timing the monotonous grinding to low-pitched songs. Others, more idle, were joining now and again in the whirling dances, with clapping of hands, thrumming of timbrels, and chanting of the vocal recitative of deeds of daring and revenge. For these were rescued wives and children, who had ridden in fear and lain in terror for the days and nights of a dreadful captivity, and now, with the spoil of the spoilers, had returned to help rebuild their ruined homes.

Within the circle of the broken wall the men toiled in joy at the task the plundering of their enemies had set them; for their revenge had been complete, and not one had lost wife or child. But as they worked, with words of cheer and blessing, the minds of many turned often with foreboding toward the northern land where they had left the hosts of Philistia and Israel confronted for battle. They were waiting anxiously for news, that seemed greatly delayed. They had been long separated from Judah, and few of Israel visited them on this edge of the desert, in a land recently annexed by the king of Gath.

The sun was nearing its meridian when over the low hills to the northeast the watchers saw a man running toward the camp. The herdboys first gave the alarm, and, amid the clamor of the camp, the warriors hastened out and gathered upon the edge of their tent-village, to await the coming messenger. That he was not an official courier was apparent from his peculiar gait, a long lope, that bespoke him of desert training rather than of the hills of Israel. He came on rapidly, evidently making an effort to finish his course with a show of zealous haste.

As he drew near, it could be seen by his appearance that the news he bore was ill: his head

As his shifty eyes strove to meet the steady gaze of the warriors

was bare, and the lank locks of hair that streamed behind him in the wind were gray with the dust of the road. His only garment, a short tunic, was torn in many places, disclosing, where it fell open in front, a breast sun-burned only less black than the swarthy face. As he sped toward them, the crowded company fell apart, leaving their chief alone in the center to receive the messenger. To him the news-bearer, slackening his pace, advanced, and fell in a profound obeisance.

"Whence comest thou?" demanded David.

"Out of the camp of Israel am I escaped," the young man answered, and paused with the evil news of his last word.

Rising, he stood facing the anxious throng, with a look that was not wholly of grief. His black face worked with an evasive emotion; his low, sloping forehead wrinkling in curious undulations as his shifty eyes strove to meet the steady gaze of the warriors. They, noting his feature by feature, saw in him an Amalekite.

He was being plied with questions by David: "How went the matter? I pray thee, tell me."

He answered, "The people are fled from the battle, and many of the people also are fallen and dead; and Saul and Jonathan his son are dead also."

"How knowest thou that Saul and Jonathan his son be dead?"

The young man's opportunity had come, he thought. He had carefully rehearsed his story for this occasion, and he prepared to make the most of it for his own advantage. With the air of the bold man his appearance belied, he told of being upon Mount Gilboa in the midst of fighting horsemen and chariots, where Saul, sorely wounded, stood leaning upon his spear. "And when he looked behind him, he saw me, and called unto me. And I answered, Here am I. And he said unto me, Who art thou? And I answered him, I am an Amalekite. He said unto me again, Stand, I pray thee, upon me, and slay me: for anguish is come upon me, because my life is yet whole in me. So I stood upon him, and slew him, because I was sure that he could not live after that he was fallen; and I took the crown that was upon his head, and the bracelet that was upon his arm, and have brought them hither unto my lord."

The Amalekite's hands had been fumbling at his girdle, and now with the last words, he drew forth a jeweled war-bonnet and a golden wrist-clasp, and reached them out to David. A scarcely concealed smile played around his mouth. His eyes were shining with the expectation of reward. The proofs of his story were in his hand: the royal insignia could not be mistaken. Saul was dead; and Jonathan was dead with him.

But neither joy nor reward came with the revelation. David rent his clothes, and with loud lamentations gave vent to a grief greater than that which four days before had filled this spot with wailings for lost wives and children. And all the men of war took up the cry; for Jonathan was dead. And the women, the singing women of an hour ago, joined their shrill trebles in the wild coronach, while frightened children whimpered and screamed, they knew not why. The passion of the East, where grief does not hide itself away, but seeks by expression to excite itself, was loosed in " sighs that are many " and " tears that run down like a river," when, " sated with wormwood and covered with ashes," they " swoon as the wounded; " " the youth and the old men lie on the ground," and " put their mouths in the dust."

The work of rebuilding was touched no more. From the ash-heaps and from within the black tents the voice of mourning and lamentation was heard through all the day till the sun was going down.

To David no greater blow had ever come.

With the hardships of an exile's life he was familiar,— with hunger, thirst, exhaustion, sleepless vigils in danger and perilous adventure in fight. He had had his home destroyed, his honors taken from him, his life treacherously attempted; he had been driven to company with wild beasts or the enemies of his people and his God; and his soul had often drunk of the wells of Marah.

But always, in injustice, deprivation, and danger, he knew there was an earthly friend who sympathized with and aided him. When the javelin waited only for his heart, Jonathan braved its point. When royal mandate declared him an outlaw and put a price upon his head, Jonathan was his advocate, and never withdrew his appeal. When dangers of hunters and of spies hemmed him in until despair seemed the only open cell, Jonathan broke through the barrier to bring courage and confidence. Arm of a warrior, hand of a maiden; brow of a master, eyes of a lover; heart whose ardor, in war and in love, had caught its flame from the altar of God; heart of Benjamin, strong in battle but gentle in peace, by whom "the beloved of the Lord should dwell in safety,"— truest type of the man of valor.

Jonathan was dead. Those cold gray heights that but few days ago the eyes of the mourner

A Man of Valor

had rested upon, those heights had drunk his blood. The hostile plain below had seen the prowess of his arm when his bow turned not in flight from mail or chariot. The treacherous heights, his own high places, the trust of Israel, had received his life from Ashkelon. The bow of Jonathan, sanctified by its association with the scene of the vow in the vale of Gibeah, the bow that had been the strength of Israel in many a hard-fought field, that bow — not in dishonor, but in glory — had at last been broken; and by "The Bow" should the name and fame of the archer of Israel be known in time to come, in Judah.

And Saul, the anointed one, slain by a base Amalekite,— on Gilboa's crags his shield was cast away. Beautiful had been the king of Israel, mighty in battle, gracious in palace hall. The wrongs that he did, they were perished; Jonathan had stood by his side, and the father was seen through the son. In life inseparable through the matchless devotion of the younger, Saul and Jonathan, as was meet, were not divided in death.

Who now should weep? Who now should mourn? Maidens, who met your king with songs and dances when he came in triumph, with spoil for your adornment, strike now the lyre in dirge for him in death.

But none, O Jonathan! can mourn for thee as David. Moons may wax and wane in glory: so the loves of common men. Suns may rise, but suns shall set; and woman's love shall not survive the grave. But long as earth shall hold on her bosom the sons of men, and, yea, beyond the reach of time, when God shall restore Eden and the Eden race, shall be known and felt the wonderful love of him who gave his life for his friend.

The sun was low, and the sounds of mourning fell with its sinking. As it paused before dipping its swollen, angry face below the dark waters of the Western sea, David stepped forth from his tent, and quickly around him there gathered the thousand souls of his encampment. At his command the Amalekite messenger, kept in custody by Abishai, was brought before him. Appalled at the tempest of grief he had aroused by his tale, the craven had cowered all the afternoon under the eye of his stern keeper. Now, as he came before the chief from whom he had expected so much as the reward of his tidings, he saw in the lowering faces that lined his path a threatened judgment, not a promised meed.

"Whence art thou?" demanded David.

He answered, "I am the son of a stranger, an Amalekite."

A Man of Valor

It was a curious scene. There stood, framed in the background of a breathless audience, the three principal actors in the tragedy: the judge, the jailer, and the prisoner. The first had twice had in his power the life of the king of Israel, and twice had refused to harm him, the Lord's anointed. The second had stood with the first at one of those times, and urged for permission himself to smite the king, and had with difficulty been restrained. The third had never been near Saul in life, but out of his own wicked, selfish heart, in the hope of reward, had invented the lie of his having killed the anointed of Israel. His doom was certain.

With stern face the judge demanded, "How wast thou not afraid to stretch forth thine hand to destroy the Lord's anointed?" Then, turning to one of his young men, David commanded, "Go near, and fall upon him." With ashen face the self-condemned man heard his sentence. He would have sunk, but the iron hand upon his arm upheld him. A sword plunged in his breast. They cast him out to the vultures of the desert. Justice walked side by side that day with Grief, and Grief leaned upon the arm of Love.

The passion of sorrow was spent, but in the travail of sorrow had been born the noblest child of song she ever bore. As the flaming torches of the sun were waving their last farewell from the watch-towers of the clouds, and the stillness of the desert's night stole in with its sacred hush, the new-made king, the stricken friend, took his harp; and, accompanied in the refrain by the voices of his people, the sweetest voice in Israel sang —

THE SONG OF THE BOW

> Thy glory, O Israel,
> Is slain upon thy high places!
> *How are the mighty —*
> *Fallen!*

Tell it not in Gath,
Publish it not in the streets of Ashkelon;
    Lest the daughters of the Philistines rejoice,
    Lest the daughters of the uncircumcised triumph.

Ye mountains of Gilboa, let there be no dew nor rain upon you,
Neither fields of offerings;
    For there the shield of the mighty was vilely cast away,
    The shield of Saul, as of one not anointed with oil!

From the blood of the slain,
From the fat of the mighty,
    The bow of Jonathan turned not back,
    And the sword of Saul returned not empty.

Saul and Jonathan were lovely and pleasant in
    their lives,
And in their death they were not divided.
  They were swifter than eagles,
  They were stronger than lions.

Ye daughters of Israel,
Weep over Saul,
  Who clothed you in scarlet delicately,
  Who put ornaments of gold upon your apparel.

>   *How are the mighty —*
>   *Fallen in the midst of the battle!*
>   *O Jonathan,*
>   *Slain upon thy high places,*

I am distressed for thee, my brother Jonathan;
Very pleasant hast thou been unto me;
  Thy love to me was wonderful,
  Passing the love of women.

>   *How are the mighty —*
>   *Fallen!*
>   *And the weapons of war —*
>   *Perished!*

CHAPTER XI

King at Last

There is a city where the light of day shall never fade, where sorrow and sighing shall never be known. The light of that city is not the light of sun nor of moon; for the light of the seven-times relumined sun is lost in the brightness of the glory of its King. The joy that men quaff there is not the mingled wine of mortal joy; for the cup is given by a Hand that has wiped the final tear. Where the waters of its river of life divide the luminous street, and the silver-golden fruit of its healing tree gleams along the margin, walk the kings of earth, every one with the coronet that tells of sovereignty and the vesture that bespeaks the priest. These are they that were redeemed from the earth, whose voices, hushed by Apollyon's hand, have been raised anew to cry, "O death, where is thy sting? O grave, where is thy victory?" whose eyes, sealed tight in the darkness that reigned from generation to generation, have opened to behold the King in his glory; whose hands, bound with the gyves of the lord of death, have been loosed to sweep the harp of the Lord of life.

A Man of Valor

For the Lord himself descended from heaven with a shout, with the voice of the Archangel, and with the trump of God; the earth trembled and shook, and the mountains flowed down at his presence. The captains of bands and the kings of nations and the great men of the earth looked up to cower beneath the eye of the King of kings. Their palaces and their towers dissolved in dust. The rock-anchored hills skipped like rams. The sea, roaring, stalked in white-crested fury over the land. Men prayed to deaf rocks to cover them, stretched imploring hands to the sheeted lightning, stopped in vain their ears from the thunder of doom. The great day of the Lord was come; who should be able to stand?

Hark! Through the shriek of the hurricane, the crash of falling crags, the terrific roar of never-ceasing thunder, rise clear and strong the tones of a triumphant song:—

> God is our refuge and strength,
>   A very present help in trouble.
> Therefore will not we fear, though the earth do change,
>   And though the mountains be moved into the heart of the seas;
> Though the waters thereof roar and be troubled,
>   Though the mountains shake with the swelling thereof.

THE LORD OF HOSTS IS WITH US:
THE GOD OF JACOB IS OUR REFUGE.

Still reeled the earth, still flamed the fire, still crashed the warring elements. Then, sweet and strong and masterful, like the sustained tones of a jubilee trumpet, the voice of the Son of God pronounced: —

> Awake! Awake! Awake!
> Ye that sleep in the dust of the earth,
> And arise.

From graves of land and sea, from battle-fields, from martyr beds on mountain peaks and plains, arose a multitude that no man could number, and joined the slender bands whose voices first had welcomed the Life-giver. Down through the cleft heavens streamed from gates ajar the glory of the celestial city; and in a mightier chorus was raised again the triumphant hymn: —

> There is a river, the streams whereof make glad the city of God,
> > The holy place of the tabernacle of the Most High.
> God is in the midst of her; she shall not be moved:
> > God shall help her at the dawning of the morning.
> The nations raged, the kings were moved:
> > He uttered his voice, the earth melted.

A Man of Valor

THE LORD OF HOSTS IS WITH US:
THE GOD OF JACOB IS OUR REFUGE.

Caught up by the word of God, the nations of the saved were ranked in the midst of legions of angels around their King. Children to mothers, sons to fathers, friends to friends, were brought by the heavenly marshals, reunited, nevermore to part. Below, the broken prison-house lay stretched in desolation. The might of the Gentile was broken. The arsenals of Abaddon were destroyed. War was ceased; for they who made war were reckoned in death with them who suffered the stroke. Nevermore should confusion and destruction reign in the hearts and lives of men. And the glorious chorus of immortals sang the final strain: —

> Come, behold the works of the Lord,
>   What desolations he hath made in the earth.
> He maketh wars to cease unto the end of the earth;
> He breaketh the bow, and cutteth the spear in sunder;
> He burneth the chariot in the fire.
> *Be still, and know that I am God:*
>   *I will be exalted among the nations,*
>   *I will be exalted in the earth.*
>
> THE LORD OF HOSTS IS WITH US:
> THE GOD OF JACOB IS OUR REFUGE.

There is a land, a radiant land of love, whose widely varied beauty is a reflection of the love that created and bestowed it. Soft, smiling skies shine down their perfect light, unveiled by tempests and unknown to droughts. No storms ever touch its fair domain, though still the winds sweep on according to their circuits, and the cool of the evening sends down the dew upon the earth to refresh it.

Plains there are of wide extent, fields of living green and gold, where the grasses and the grains dip and wave, dip and wave, in joyous accord with the universal homage paid to the great King. The little hills that bound them give a fringe of varied color, with the white of the lily and the crimson of the rose. Purple is no exclusive royal color there, and the hyacinth mingles with the buttercup to make a crown of glory for the hills. Upward goes the path of the eye, range after range of hills swelling higher to merge in the noble crested heights; for the mountains there are not rough, jagged upheavals, with outcroppings of ledge and cliff, but beautiful slopes of living green, flower-besprinkled and tree-bedecked, whose heights give prospects over many leagues, with every hill and lake and field and vine-roofed palace clear and distinct through the limpid air.

There are watercourses and systems wonderful to contemplate. The great, wide, rolling waste of ocean is no more, but there are expanses of water through which the rivers run. Sparkling and clear as rivers never seen, they carry life and gladness everywhere they go. Like unknown rivers, too, their relations — not flowing all to join one common sea, but uniting, dividing, expanding, hiding; flowing here a broad, serene river through the plain, there tinkling in little rills in hidden dales, here bursting into hill-girt lakes and flowing out again to join their brother rivulets, now dashing under hills to emerge elsewhere in sparkling springs; singing, laughing, sedately flowing, always blessing, always clear and bright, blue in the depths and like sunshine and air in the shallows. O beautiful River of Life, that, issuing forth from the throne of God, shall cause everything to live whithersoever thou comest! For this is the land of the world redeemed,— the great, the glad, the glorious New Earth.

Here is the kingdom of Israel; for all the earth shall be Israel in that day. Here is the city of the New Jerusalem, the city of the Prince of peace. And from every quarter of its wide domain, Sabbath by Sabbath and every new moon, come up the tribes of the Lord for a testimony to Israel, and to give thanks unto the name of the Lord.

Just to the south of the wide zone in which the great capital is situated, lies the land of Benjamin; and beyond, Simeon, Issachar, Zebulon, and Gad. Each by his nature (all of which combine to make the perfect character of King Jesus), the redeemed sons of earth have been allotted to their tribes. Organized like the angelic hosts, the tribes of the Lord, though every member is a king, have heads of families and governors of tribes — kings in pre-eminence. They who in patient and virile perseverance have been the chief, are fathers of the tribe of Gad; they the greatest of the burden-bearers, rule over Zebulon and Issachar.

And Benjamin, the chivalrous — unblenching and daring in the wars of the Lord, gracious and tender to the unprotected — of the great hearts of Benjamin shall we know the king? Shall it be that dauntless man who nailed the challenge of God on the doors of Rome, and fought forward with never sheathed sword until the field was cleared; and yet whose bosom held matchless pity for the weak, and love for little children? Shall it be that heroic apostle whose banner was planted where the savage Crescent ruled; who, single-handed against ten thousands of foes, in blood and famine, in nakedness and distress, carried the name of his Prince and the heraldcry of His coming until all the Moslem world had heard the fame? Shall it be that hero of Tarsus, whose fiery zeal could not be quenched by stonings or stripes, by perils on the land or perils in the sea, by hunger or thirst, by cold or nakedness, by imprisonments or by threats of death; but who, glorying in infirmities wherein he was made strong, took stronghold after stronghold, until the world fell before Christ? Or shall it be the prototype of them all, Jonathan — who through faith subdued kingdoms, wrought righteousness, obtained promises, turned aside the edge of the sword, out of weakness was made strong, waxed valiant in fight, turned to flight the armies of the aliens; who sought not his own glory, but of his friend could say with perfect peace, "He must increase, but I must decrease;" and who sealed his testimony with the perfect test his Master gave,— " Greater love hath no man than this, that a man lay down his life for his friend"?

The families of earth are gathering to the Sabbath service. From the garden-homes of Eden they come, great armies, mightier in numbers than the biggest hosts ever marshaled on old earth, and incomparable in power and glory. As the companies of Benjamin gather along the paths, how the names and deeds of the great throng the memory! From south and east and west they come whom in time we knew by mortal names — Jonathan, Ehud, Esther, Paul, and many another of apostles and evangelists, missionaries and explorers, councilors and warriors. Joined by innumerable companies from the south, the glorious processions sweep along toward the New Jerusalem.

The approach to the city is through the most varied and beautiful scenes. Through forests of illumined palms, oaks, cedars, firs, the pilgrims take their ways, now walking amid groves of citrus, apple, pomegranate, and all manner of fruits; now examining the vineyards, whose plants rear their graceful heads without support. Thus through the estates of the immortal they pass, their ranks continually swelling with the households and families who from the silver-columned palaces come forth with one mind to keep the holy festal day.

Cascades along the way fall over ledges, not of broken, somber rock, but of gleaming quartz, of gold and silver, and of many-colored stones.

A Man of Valor

Fountains jet and throw their feathery forms aloft in the sunshine, catching in their arms, as they rise and descend, the swiftly playing colors of the rainbow, like that which spans the throne. On bridges of crystal and gold, magnificently wrought, the throngs cross the streams that throw their network about the city of God; and finally they cross that wondrous sea of glass that spreads before the gates of the city.

From every quarter the people of earth are drawing near. Music of voice and instrument, inconceivable in harmony, rises from every pilgrim band, as, topping the heights of the gently sloping mountains, they pause to gaze upon that glorious city, set like a jasper jewel in the green fields of Eden.

They enter the city through twelve great gates, three on each side, upon each the name of one of the tribes. A majestic angel warder stands at the gateway, not as a guard, but as a sign of heaven's order transplanted here. Each tribe to its gate: from the south the Benjamites sweep around to the east, to enter the southernmost of those three gates, next to the entrance ways of Ephraim and Manasseh; the Gadites part to the left, to enter a gate upon the west side; while the men of Simeon, Isaachar, and Zebulon enter the three gates upon the south which bear their names; from the north, Reuben and Judah come down, and are joined upon the north side of the city by the Levites, and each enters its own gate; and the two northernmost tribes, Asher and Naphtali, have their gates upon the west side, next to that of Gad, though between them flows out the beautiful River of Life.

The heads of the columns have crossed the shining crystal sea, and have entered through the pearly gates into the glorious jeweled garden-city.

>I was glad when they said unto me,
>Let us go unto the house of the Lord.
>>Our feet are standing within thy gates, O Jerusalem.
>>Jerusalem, thou art builded as a city that is compact together:
>
>Whither the tribes go up, even the tribes of the Lord,
>For a testimony unto Israel, to give thanks unto the name of the Lord.
>>For there are set thrones of judgment,
>>The thrones of the house of David.
>
>Pray for the peace of Jerusalem:
>They shall prosper that love thee.
>>Peace be within thy walls,
>>And prosperity within thy palaces.

> For my brethren and companions' sakes,
> I will now say, Peace be within thee.
>> For the sake of the house of the Lord our God,
>> I will seek thy good.

Through the broad avenues, the distances and spaces of which we can not estimate, the glad throngs pour. Set in the midst of gardens are the palaces, wonderful homes built by the hand of God, with precious stones for garniture of their golden, transparent walls, within which darkness never reigns, and from which the vine and the flower are not shut out. Their domes and minarets shine in the glory of One that is greater than the sun, a light from the throne whence issues the River of Life. There the redeemed are gathered; and before the ineffable glory of their King they bow themselves, and cast down their crowns in adoring love, hailing him Root of David, Lion of the tribe of Judah, Lamb of God:—

"Worthy is the Lamb that was slain to receive power, and riches, and wisdom, and strength, and honor, and glory, and blessing."

"Salvation to our God, which sitteth upon the throne, and unto the Lamb."

And the angels that in uncounted legions throng the throne, fall before the King upon their faces, crying:—

"Amen! Blessing, and glory, and wisdom, and thanksgiving, and honor, and power, and might, be unto our God forever and ever. Amen!"

And that King who in the days of Galilee and Judea walked and talked with men; who bore their weaknesses and their sins; who soothed the grief-stricken and calmed the sorrowing; in whose arms the children lay and gazed upon his face in love; on whose breast reposed the head of many a weary earth-wanderer; who gave food to the famishing and salvation to the lost — that King now is to his people the same. With them he talks; to them he gives renewed life; for them he plucks the fruit of life; to them he hands the wine of the grapes of the kingdom; for them he divides the manna of heaven.

Around their great Sovereign the kings of the earth gather closely, mingling with his nearest followers, the Brands-from-the-Burning and the Redeemed-from-among-Men. There is Peter, who found his love in humiliation. There is Elijah, who watched with God through half of time the consummation of salvation. There is Abraham, the father of the faithful; and Jacob, whose fight of faith won him the name of the nation. There is Paul, from persecutor made apostle; Luther, mighty in the pulling down of strongholds;

A Man of Valor

Livingstone, whose message-written heart has seen its answer. There is the herald of Immanuel, John the Baptist, type in the new dispensation of the perfect friend, as Jonathan in the old.

And there, bright in the glory of immortal men, is the shepherd-musician of Bethlehem, the captain of Judah, the king of Israel, the man after God's own heart, David. Before him stands the soul-knit friend of his earthly days, who, " bound with him in the bundle of life with the Lord their God," though parted from him long, shall be parted now no more. Not less than the love of mortal days is the love of immortal ages. Sharp was the warfare, and long it seemed; but the worn warriors will never need to fight again. Jonathan, " Whom Jehovah Gave," Jehovah has received again, and for the wormwood of the mortal life has given the balm of the immortal. Gone forever are the days of toil and the nights of watching; banished the evil and the bitterness. No more the morning calls to war's alarms, and the night to war's councils. For day invites to peaceful labor, wherein lies the learning of the wise, and night is eloquent to teach the wonders of the universe.

Earth's discipline has vanished in heaven's delights. The man of valor has become a king of grace. The benison of a heavenly peace, the joy of an eternal life, the love of a marless brotherhood, the glory of kinship with God, have been the fruit of the days of suffering and denial. The hand of God has closed the gates of time. The feet of the sons of God tread now the way that is from everlasting to everlasting.

Out from the dust of the past, out from the gloom of time, the ransomed of the Lord arise; they shine as the brightness of the firmament, as the stars forever and ever. And, in answer to the voice of their King,—

"Comfort ye, comfort ye my people, saith your God. Speak ye comfortably to Jerusalem, and cry unto her, that her warfare is accomplished, that her iniquity is pardoned,"—

the great choir of earth and heaven makes response in the rhapsody of "Zion Redeemed:"—

The Celestial Hosts

Awake, awake; put on thy strength, O Zion;
Put on thy beautiful garments, O Jerusalem, the holy city;
For henceforth there shall no more come into thee the uncircumcised and the unclean.

A Man of Valor

Shake thyself from the dust;
Arise, sit thee down, O Jerusalem;
Loose thyself from the bands of thy neck, O captive daughter of Zion."

Chorus of the Redeemed

How beautiful upon the mountains are the feet of him
  That bringeth good tidings, that publisheth peace;
  That bringeth good tidings of good, that publisheth salvation;
That saith unto Zion, Thy God reigneth!

The voice of thy Watchmen! They lift up the voice,
  Together do they sing;
  For they shall see, eye to eye,
How the Lord returneth to Zion.

Break forth into joy, sing together,
  Ye waste places of Jerusalem;
For the Lord hath comforted his people,
  He hath redeemed Jerusalem.

The Lord hath made bare his holy arm
  In the eyes of all the nations,
  And all the ends of the earth
Shall see the salvation of our God.

THE END

APPENDIX

An After-Word

The author has not thought that those of the class and age for whom this book is intended, would be swift to inquire the purpose of its being written. For this reason he has deemed it unnecessary to place before them what would be considered by many a useless preface. But if the book has accomplished any of its very real purpose, the readers will be likely to seek as far as this note for information which would before have been valueless.

It has not been to add a pleasant tale to the multitude so much better told, that "A Man of Valor" has been written, nor to furnish the careless reader something to take in any part the place of the Book from which this has been mostly drawn. But its purpose has been to illustrate the author's belief that the stories of the Bible, if lived over in the imagination, and connected with the knowledge of local geography, customs, and manners, which may be gotten by every reader, will have a charm beyond that of the stories of any other nation or people. Because they hold up for approbation the noblest traits of character, and for condemnation the evil that so often clings thereto; because, while they faithfully portray the oftentimes sordid motives of the men they picture, they yet present as correct incentives the highest conceptions of duty and pleasure; because in their narration they keep ever in sight the overruling power of God in the affairs of men, and point always to his certain reward of good or evil, — the Bible stories are unequaled in narrative literature for power to form sturdy, useful, and noble souls. Because they are told simply, without that obtrusion of the personality of the narrator which only the masters are able to avoid; and because, containing only the truth, they are altogether free from the many discrepancies and other faults which mar the pages of fiction,— they have a freshness, a convincing charm of expression, which always takes captive the heart and mind of the appreciative reader.

It is because the Bible is regarded by many children and youth only as a storehouse of piety, that it is so widely dreaded and shunned. Whosever the fault of this,— whether of dogmatic teachers or of ignorant companions,— every one who will come to the books of the Bible as to a storehouse of literary entertainment, and who will read, not as a task, but leisurely, with a mind that lives in what it receives, will be sure to find the Bible a delightful friend and instructor. And if he wishes to become better able to appreciate its stories, and to get from it vivid pictures, let him devote a little time to solid study of the geography of Palestine, of the dress, architecture, and arts of its people in ancient times, and of their social and religious customs. These may all be found within one handbook; or, if the student will go further, he will find a whole library of works upon these subjects.

The effect of such reading and such study will be not merely to give information upon the subject of Biblical literature (to be in ignorance of which is a disgrace), but, more than that, to furnish and inspire an originality of thought and expression which the youth may otherwise seek in vain. The Bible has been the food that chiefly nourished the most of our greatest English authors; and its influence in literature can be clearly but only partly traced in the Biblical figures and allusions and themes which we find so profuse in the works of the masters.

To furnish an illustration of what such study offers to every young man or woman who will rightly use his imagination, and make such researches, has been the purpose of the writing of

"A Man of Valor." It will be noted that no fictitious name nor character has been introduced into the narrative, and that the imagination has been used only to amplify and make more vivid the pictures presented by the sacred narrative, combined with our knowledge of Bible manners, customs, and geography. This is the legitimate work of the imagination, and care need be had only in guarding against going contrary to known fact, and against entering the realm of the improbable.

If the life of Jonathan, thus presented, appeals to the reader, let him remember that there are hundreds of other stories, romantic and beautiful in differing and varying degrees, which he may himself create from the pages of the Bible. And to this, rather than to a dependence upon some chance writer, the author would urge his friends, the readers. To help them in making this start, or in pursuing it further if already made, he has given the above suggestions, and will add a list of a few of the books which, obtained from libraries or by purchase, will make them stronger, abler, and more enthusiastic Bible readers.

For a book which combines the most valuable information in the smallest compass, "Sacred Geography and Antiquities," by Rev. R. P. Barrows (publishers, American Tract Society, New York), may stand at the head of the list. Other works which will be found helpful are: —

Robinson's "Biblical Researches in Palestine," 3 volumes.

Porter's "Giant Cities of Bashan, and Syria's Holy Places."

Stanley's "Sinai and Palestine."

Thomson's "Land and the Book," 3 volumes.

Maspero's "Ancient Egypt and Assyria."

Wilkinson's "Ancient Egyptians."

Sayce's "Assyria: Its Princes, Priests, and People."

Dawson's "Egypt and Syria."

Guhl and Koner's "Life of the Greeks and Romans."

Freeman's "Handbook of Bible Manners and Customs."

Edersheim's "Temple: Its Ministry and Services."

Kitto's "Bible Illustrations," 8 volumes.

Geike's "Hours with the Bible," 6 volumes.

Any of the standard Bible dictionaries and encyclopedias.

The verse and chapter structure of the Authorized Version of the Bible is not a little confusing, and oftentimes destructive of interest. The use of the American Revised Version will be found advantageous, not less on this account than because of its greater accuracy. A still better rendering is given in the "Modern Reader's Bible," edited by Prof. R. G. Moulton, and published by the Macmillan Company, New York. In this the literary structure of the Bible compositions — poems, stories, essays, dramas, etc.— are given in the forms which modern literary works always take. The author would here acknowledge his indebtedness to the publishers of the "Modern Reader's Bible" for permission to use its structure forms in a number of psalms and other passages which have been quoted.

That many, through reading this book, may feel themselves to have been made more really acquainted with one of the most beautiful characters history knows, and inspired so to live that they may be worthy to clasp hands with him in the earth redeemed; and that some may be helped to a deeper and more appreciative study of the Book of books, which is the fountain-head of great thoughts and great deeds, is the hope of —

THE AUTHOR.

Berrien Springs, Mich., Jan. 28, 1906.

Notes

NOTE 1.— The length of Saul's reign is a disputed question. The Old Testament does not tell it; but in Acts 13:21 Stephen says that "afterward they desired a king; and God gave unto them Saul the son of Cis, a man of the tribe of Benjamin, by the space of forty years." This "forty years," however, may include the judgeship of Samuel, which is mentioned in the preceding verse.

The chief objections to thinking the reign of Saul to have been so long as forty years may be briefly stated as follows: —

(*a*) When Saul was crowned king, his son Jonathan was old enough to be engaged in war; but at his death, Jonathan's son, Mephibosheth, was only five years old. If forty years had intervened, Jonathan would then have been about sixty years old, and would have become a father only at the age of fifty-five, which is unlikely.

(*b*) David at his accession was thirty years old. If Jonathan was then sixty, he would have been forty-five or fifty at the time he first met David, and David only fifteen or twenty. But the friendship of David and Jonathan is too evidently that of young men to admit of this.

(*c*) The impressions of Saul's reign made by the narrative in First Samuel is that the events follow one another somewhat closely, and by their fewness indicate a short reign.

For these and other reasons, Bliss, in "Sacred Chronology," inclines to think that the "forty years" in Acts 13:21 cover both the judgeship of Samuel and the reign of Saul; that Saul reigned no more than twenty years; and that Jonathan and Saul at the time of their death were in age forty-two and sixty years respectively.

NOTE 2.— The site of Nob has not been satisfactorily identified by travelers, but Porter ("Giant Cities of Bashan," page 185), believed that he had found the spot, and his statement is taken for the basis of its location in this book.

NOTE 3.— Adonizedec and the kings who joined with him against the Gibeonites are said (Joshua 10:5) to have been kings of the Amorites. The kingdom of Bashan was a kingdom of the Amorites, and was ruled over by Og, of the giant race. Deut. 3:8-11. This relation of the Anakim, or giants, to the Amorites seems to have given the latter the reputation of being a giant race. Amos 2:9. Two at least of the cities confederate with Adonizedec are said to have been the dwelling-place of the Anakim. Joshua 11:21. While these facts favor the supposition that Adonizedec and his confederates were giants, it can not, however, be said to be a certainty.

NOTE 4.— The site of Ramah, the home of Samuel, is not agreed upon by travelers. Ramah — "a high place" — as the name of a town, occurs frequently in the Bible, and there were evidently a number of different places so named. Ramah in Benjamin has been located by Robinson ("Biblical Researches," Vol. I, page 576), at the modern Er-Ram, three miles northeast of the site of Gibeah. Most authorities, while accepting this identification, reject it as being Ramah the home of Samuel, on the ground of the passage in 1 Sam. 9:5-10, 13, where we are told that in a city in "the land of Zuph" Saul found Samuel, and in the prediction of the prophet of what should happen to him on his way home, he was told

Appendix

that he should go "by Rachel's sepulcher in the border of Benjamin." This fixes the location of the city where Samuel was,— and which is generally assumed to have been his home, Ramah — to the south of Gibeah and Bethlehem. There is little in the text, however, to denote that this city was Samuel's home, and therefore Ramah; and if this supposition is done away with, there is not only no objection against, but a number of reasons for, supposing Samuel's home and Ramah in Benjamin to have been the same. Several writers (Pocock, Bachiene, Raumer, Winer) have held this to be true. Upon this well-founded supposition, therefore, Ramah, the home of Samuel, is assumed in this book to be Ramah of Benjamin.

NOTE 5.— The law of blood revenge was an ancient and passionate form of executing justice upon a murderer. The nearest relative of the murdered person was bound to find the murderer and kill him. This law, universal among ancient Eastern peoples, was in the Israelite mind so deep-seated and so wrapped up with the sense of justice, that when God gave them the law in the wilderness, he did not try to abolish it, but rather put around it such limitations as to make its abuse impossible.

When the land of Canaan was divided among the tribes, six cities, three on each side Jordan, were set apart as "cities of refuge," to which the man-slayer might flee, and within which, if his crime should be proved not to be worthy of death, he might be safe. Upon the death of the high priest he should be free to return home, and be safe from the vengeance of the blood-revenger.

On the west of Jordan, Hebron was the southern city of refuge, and Shechem the central. To make easy the escape of the slayer, the roads from every direction, leading to the city of refuge, were required to be kept in the best condition, and sign-posts were erected at all the junctions of roads, showing the way to the cities of refuge. As the main mountain road between Hebron and Shechem lay through the valley below Gibeah, this is doubtless the meaning of what in the text is called "the stone Ezel," and by interpretation in the margin, "the stone which showeth the way."

NOTE 6.— The Korhites were descendants of Korah, the Levite, who, rebelling against the government under Moses, was swallowed up when the earth opened. But his children were not included in his destruction.

While the priests and Levites had distinctively a peaceful work assigned them, we nevertheless find them not infrequently engaging in battle, along with their brethren of other tribes. Some of David's most famous warriors were Levites; and at various other times of trouble we catch glimpses of armed Levites. They were, however, in the army most frequently as trumpeters and exhorters, and usually fought only in extremity.

NOTE 7.— Ebenezer means "stone of help;" "for hitherto hath the Lord helped us." Aphek means "strength." The names are found in connection in 1 Samuel 4, where the Israelites pitched in Aphek. These places were in Benjamin, or possibly in Dan or Judah, in the southwestern part of the land. There were, however, a number of other places named Aphek, and one of these was in the valley of Jezreel, where the Philistines pitched against Saul.

When the Philistines pitched in Aphek against Israel in the days of Eli, they were victorious in the battle which followed; when they came against the Israelites

Appendix

in the time of Samuel, they were defeated, and Ebenezer received its name from that defeat. Thus, Ebenezer may be taken as symbolic of Hebrew victory, and Aphek of Philistine triumph; though the Aphek of 1 Samuel 4 and that of 1 Samuel 29 are to be distinguished.

TEACH Services, Inc.
P U B L I S H I N G

We invite you to view the complete
selection of titles we publish at:
www.TEACHServices.com

We encourage you to write us
with your thoughts about this,
or any other book we publish at:
info@TEACHServices.com

TEACH Services' titles may be purchased in
bulk quantities for educational, fund-raising,
business, or promotional use.
bulksales@TEACHServices.com

Finally, if you are interested in seeing
your own book in print, please contact us at:
publishing@TEACHServices.com

We are happy to review your manuscript at no charge.

INDEX TO CHAPTERS

CHAPTER		PAGE
I.	A Perilous Situation .	7
II.	Not by Many, but by Few	21
III.	Honey and Blood .	35
IV.	The Beginning of Evil	57
V.	The Cleaving of Souls	84
VI.	Intercessor and Defender	110
VII.	In Palace and Wood	139
VIII.	A Night of Gloom	165
IX.	Gilboa .	181
X.	The Song of the Bow	209
XI.	King at Last	220
Appendix .		237

World rights reserved. This book or any portion thereof may not be copied or reproduced in any form or manner whatever, except as provided by law, without the written permission of the publisher, except by a reviewer who may quote brief passages in a review.

The author assumes full responsibility for the accuracy of all facts and quotations as cited in this book. The opinions expressed in this book are the author's personal views and interpretations, and do not necessarily reflect those of the publisher.

This book is provided with the understanding that the publisher is not engaged in giving spiritual, legal, medical, or other professional advice. If authoritative advice is needed, the reader should seek the counsel of a competent professional.

Facsimile Reproduction

As this book played a formative role in the development of Christian thought and the publisher feels that this book, with its candor and depth, still holds significance for the church today. Therefore the publisher has chosen to reproduce this historical classic from an original copy. Frequent variations in the quality of the print are unavoidable due to the condition of the original. Thus the print may look darker or lighter or appear to be missing detail, more in some places than in others.

Copyright © 2023 TEACH Services, Inc.
ISBN-13: 978-1-4796-1663-3 (Paperback)

Published by

www.TEACHServices.com • (800) 367-1844

A Man of Valor

By ARTHUR W. SPALDING

*A Story of the Life of Jonathan
Son of Saul*

TEACH Services, Inc.
PUBLISHING
www.TEACHServices.com • (800) 367-1844

www.ingramcontent.com/pod-product-compliance
Lightning Source LLC
Chambersburg PA
CBHW071147160426
43196CB00011B/2032